AF791596

Lynda Ait Bachir

Foundations of Financial Markets:

Lynda Ait Bachir

Foundations of Financial Markets:

Analysis and Strategies for Financial Portfolio Management

Noor Publishing

Imprint
Any brand names and product names mentioned in this book are subject to trademark, brand or patent protection and are trademarks or registered trademarks of their respective holders. The use of brand names, product names, common names, trade names, product descriptions etc. even without a particular marking in this work is in no way to be construed to mean that such names may be regarded as unrestricted in respect of trademark and brand protection legislation and could thus be used by anyone.

Cover image: www.ingimage.com

Publisher:
Noor Publishing
is a trademark of
Dodo Books Indian Ocean Ltd. and OmniScriptum S.R.L publishing group

120 High Road, East Finchley, London, N2 9ED, United Kingdom
Str. Armeneasca 28/1, office 1, Chisinau MD-2012, Republic of Moldova, Europe
Managing Directors: Ieva Konstantinova, Victoria Ursu
info@omniscriptum.com

Printed at: see last page
ISBN: 978-620-8-87088-1

Foundations of Financial Markets: Analysis and Strategies for Financial Portfolio Management

Prepared by Dr LYNDA AIT BACHIR

Dedication

This book is dedicated to all the students, researchers, and practitioners who strive to deepen their understanding of financial markets and portfolio management. May this work serve as a valuable resource on your journey toward knowledge and success in the world of finance.

Contents

Introduction

It is with great gratitude and enthusiasm that we present this work titled "Foundations of Financial Markets: Analysis and Strategies for Financial Portfolio Management". This book has been crafted with the objective of offering comprehensive insights into the fundamental principles of financial investment, the structures and functions of financial markets, and effective strategies for managing financial portfolios. It serves as a resource for both students and researchers, providing the tools and knowledge required to navigate the complexities of the financial world.

As the author, my aim is to bridge the gap between theory and practice in the field of financial markets and portfolio management. The goal is to equip readers with a deep understanding of the various financial instruments, market structures, and portfolio management strategies, while also exploring the models and evaluation methods used to assess the performance of financial portfolios. This book has been designed to provide valuable guidance for anyone looking to gain a strong foundation in finance.

This book is structured into eight chapters, each focusing on a specific aspect of financial markets and portfolio management.

Chapter One" Principles of Financial Investment" :This opening chapter introduces the concept of financial investment, explaining its fundamental principles and key characteristics. It highlights the main objectives of financial investment, the different areas in which investments can be made, and the advantages and risks associated with financial investments. The chapter aims to build a solid foundation for understanding the core principles of investing in financial markets.

Chapter Two" Introduction to Financial Markets": In this chapter, we delve into the definition and importance of financial markets, along with a discussion on the various participants involved. We also explore the functions of the capital market and the structure of financial markets. This chapter provides readers with an essential understanding of how financial markets operate and their significance in the global economy.

Chapter Three "Financial Market Instruments" this chapter focuses on the various financial instruments available in the market, such as money market instruments and capital market instruments. It explains the features and roles of these instruments, giving readers an understanding of how they are used in investment strategies. This chapter covers the different markets, including the money market and capital market, and the instruments that drive them.

Chapter Four "Financial Market Efficiency" :In this chapter, we define financial market efficiency and explore its different types, such as strong-form and economic efficiency. The chapter discusses the assumptions underlying the Efficient Market Hypothesis (EMH) and highlights some of the key criticisms of this hypothesis. Additionally, alternative theories and models of market efficiency are examined to offer a balanced perspective on the topic.

Chapter Five "An Introduction to Investment Portfolios" : Chapter five provides an introduction to investment portfolios, discussing their origins and importance in financial management. It covers the different types and objectives of investment portfolios, as well as the factors and controls necessary when building a portfolio. This chapter introduces the foundational concepts that underpin effective portfolio construction and the considerations involved in selecting the right investments.

Chapter Six "Portfolio Management and Administration Strategies": this chapter explores the objectives and methods of portfolio management, focusing on the various strategies that portfolio managers use to optimize returns while managing risk. It covers the decision-making processes involved in managing portfolios, hedging strategies, and the policies and steps necessary for successful portfolio administration. The chapter also highlights key factors to consider when making portfolio management decisions.

Chapter Seven "Financial Portfolio Models": In this chapter, we explore various financial portfolio models that help in constructing and managing portfolios effectively. Topics such as efficient and optimal portfolios, the Sharpe and Johnson market models, and the Capital Asset Pricing Model (CAPM) are discussed. The chapter also covers other key models, including the Security Market Line (SML), the Capital Market Line (CML), the Fama-French 3 Factor Model, and Arbitrage Pricing Theory (APT).

Chapter Eight" Portfolio Performance Evaluation": The final chapter delves into the principles of evaluating portfolio performance. It explores several performance evaluation models, including the Sharpe Model (1966), Treynor's Performance Measure (1965), the Johnson Model (1968), the Fama Model, and the Henrikson-Merton Model. The chapter also addresses obstacles in performance measurement and offers a comprehensive discussion on how to effectively assess the success of financial portfolios.

While every effort has been made to ensure the accuracy and depth of the content within this book, we acknowledge that there may be areas that require further elaboration or refinement. We humbly offer our apologies for any potential shortcomings or gaps in the material. Our goal has always been to provide a thorough and insightful resource for those seeking to deepen their understanding of financial markets and portfolio management.

We hope that this book will prove to be a useful guide for students, academics, and professionals alike, assisting them in their studies and practice in the dynamic field of finance.

Chapter One
Principles of Financial Investment

Chapter One: Principles of Financial Investment

Financial investment is a cornerstone of wealth creation and economic growth. It involves allocating resources typically in the form of money into various financial assets or ventures, with the expectation of generating a return over time. The principles that govern financial investment help investors manage risk, maximise returns, and achieve their long-term financial goals. This chapter introduces the concept of financial investment, explores its significance, and provides a comprehensive overview of the types of investments available to individuals and institutions alike.

1.1 Definition of Financial Investment

Financial investment refers to the act of allocating capital or resources to financial assets or ventures (e.g., stocks, bonds, real estate) with the expectation of generating returns over time. It involves risk management and strategic decisions to optimize long-term capital appreciation, income generation, or a combination of both.

1.2 Key characteristics of financial investment

This section highlights the fundamental characteristics that define financial investments and influence decision-making processes in investment strategies.

- **Liquidity**: Liquidity refers to the ease with which an investment can be converted into cash without significantly affecting its price. More liquid investments, like stocks or bonds, can be sold quickly, whereas others, like real estate, may take longer to sell and are less liquid.
- **Diversification:** Diversification is the practice of spreading investments across various asset classes (e.g., stocks, bonds, real estate) to reduce risk. By diversifying,

investors can minimize the impact of a poor-performing asset on the overall investment portfolio.

- **Time Horizon:** The time horizon refers to the length of time an investor expects to hold an investment before taking the money out. Short-term investments generally involve lower risk and offer lower returns, while long-term investments tend to have higher risk but the potential for higher returns over time.
- **Economic Impact:** Financial investments play a crucial role in driving economic growth by channeling funds into productive uses, such as infrastructure development, technological innovations, and business expansions. The direction of investments often reflects broader economic trends and can influence market stability.

1.3 Objectives of Financial Investment

The objectives of financial investment are multifaceted and essential for investors seeking to achieve specific financial goals, which will be elaborated upon in detail below.

- **Achieving Financial Returns :** Financial investment is considered one of the most efficient ways to allocate funds, as it helps investors achieve their goals. This includes adopting balanced policies, such as investing in financial assets that offer high returns with a relatively low degree of risk.
- **Continuous Wealth Development:** The objective is to generate an acceptable return, with a reasonable increase in the value of invested capital over the long term, ensuring sustained wealth growth.
- **Protecting Capital from Depreciation:** Financial investment serves as a means to protect funds from the adverse effects of inflation and the fluctuations in purchasing power, thus securing the value of money over time.

- **Increasing Investment in Financial Markets:** Financial investments enhance an individual's or institution's capacity to interact with both local and international financial markets, fostering greater market participation.
- **Preserving Income from Taxes:** Through various strategies, investors can benefit from tax advantages, which may improve the overall returns from their investments.

1.4 Areas of Financial Investment

This section explores the key areas of financial investment, each with its unique characteristics, risk profiles, and potential for returns.

- **Stock Market Investments (Equity Investments):** Stock market investments involve purchasing shares (also known as equities) in publicly listed companies. By doing so, investors gain partial ownership in a company, allowing them to benefit from its growth. This growth can be in the form of dividends (periodic profit distributions) and capital appreciation (increase in stock price). Stocks are considered a relatively higher-risk investment compared to bonds, but they offer the potential for higher returns over the long term.
  Key Features:
  - Investors have the potential for both capital gains and income through dividends.
  - The value of the investment is directly tied to the company's performance and the market's response to it.
  - Stocks can be volatile, meaning prices can fluctuate significantly based on market conditions.
- **Bond Investments (Fixed Income Investments):** Bond investments involve lending money to governments, municipalities, or corporations in exchange for regular

interest payments (coupons) and the return of the principal amount at the bond's maturity. Bonds are typically considered less risky than stocks, as they offer a fixed return and have a predetermined maturity date.

Key Features:

- Bonds are generally considered lower-risk investments compared to stocks.
- They provide predictable income through interest payments.
- The value of a bond can be affected by interest rates, inflation, and the creditworthiness of the issuer.

• **Real Estate Investments:** Real estate investments involve purchasing properties with the aim of generating income through rent or selling the property for a profit after it appreciates in value. Real estate can be an attractive investment, as it provides a tangible asset that can act as a hedge against inflation. There are two main types of real estate investment:
    - Residential Property: Investing in homes or apartments for rental income or resale.
    - Commercial Property: Investing in office buildings, retail spaces, or industrial properties, which typically provide a higher return on investment.

  Key Features:
    - Real estate provides both income and capital appreciation.
    - Property values can be influenced by location, economic conditions, and market trends.
    - Real estate is a long-term investment that can be illiquid, meaning it may take time to sell.

• **Mutual Funds and Exchange-Traded Funds (ETFs):** Mutual funds and ETFs pool money from various investors to invest in a diversified portfolio of stocks, bonds, or other assets. Mutual funds are typically managed

by professional portfolio managers, while ETFs trade on exchanges like stocks and usually track specific indices.
Key Features:

- Mutual funds and ETFs offer diversification, spreading risk across different asset classes.
- They are less risky than investing in individual stocks as they involve a broader range of investments.
- ETFs generally have lower fees than mutual funds and can be bought and sold like stocks.

- **Commodities Investments:** Commodities investments involve trading raw materials or primary agricultural products such as gold, oil, or wheat. Investors can invest directly in the commodities themselves or through commodity-related financial instruments like futures contracts and commodity ETFs. Commodities are often seen as a hedge against inflation and economic instability.
  Key Features:
  - Commodities can be volatile and influenced by geopolitical events, supply and demand, and weather conditions.
  - They do not provide income in the form of dividends or interest, but can offer capital gains if prices rise.
  - Commodities are typically used to diversify portfolios and hedge against market downturns.
- **Alternative Investments** :Alternative investments include a broad range of non-traditional assets such as hedge funds, private equity, venture capital, and collectibles (e.g., art, wine, and antiques). These investments are typically less liquid and may require a larger capital outlay, but they can offer high returns.
  Key Features:
  - Alternative investments are often used by high-net-worth individuals and institutional investors.

- They can provide diversification by adding assets that are not correlated with traditional stock and bond markets.
- These investments often come with higher risks and lower liquidity.

- **Cryptocurrencies and Digital Assets:** Cryptocurrencies such as Bitcoin and Ethereum have emerged as a new form of digital investment. These digital currencies operate on blockchain technology and are decentralised, meaning they are not controlled by a central authority like a government or bank. Cryptocurrencies can be highly volatile and speculative but have attracted significant interest from both individual and institutional investors.
  Key Features:
  - Cryptocurrencies are speculative investments, and their value can fluctuate widely.
  - They offer a new form of digital asset with the potential for high returns but come with significant risks.
  - The regulatory environment surrounding cryptocurrencies is still evolving, which adds uncertainty.

1.5 Principles of Financial Investment

The principles of financial investment form the backbone of successful investment strategies. These principles are essential for making informed decisions, optimising returns, and managing risk effectively. Understanding these core concepts is fundamental for anyone engaging in the investment process, whether as an individual investor or as a financial institution. Below are the key principles that guide the world of financial investment:

- **Risk and Return:** The risk-return trade-off is a central concept in investment. It posits that higher returns are generally associated with higher risk. In other words, investors must take on more risk if they expect to achieve higher returns. Conversely, lower-risk investments tend to offer lower returns. This principle underscores the need for investors to assess their risk tolerance and choose investments that align with their financial goals and risk appetite.

- Risk refers to the possibility of losing money or seeing a reduction in the value of an investment.
- Return represents the profit or income generated from the investment, typically expressed as a percentage of the original amount invested.

- **Time Value of Money (TVM):** The Time Value of Money is one of the most fundamental principles in investment theory. It asserts that money available today is worth more than the same amount of money in the future due to its potential to earn a return. This principle is vital for evaluating investment opportunities, as it considers the opportunity cost of waiting to receive a certain sum of money.
  - TVM is used in evaluating cash flows, determining present and future values, and assessing the attractiveness of different investment options.
  - It highlights the importance of compounding returns and how reinvesting profits over time can significantly increase the value of an investment.
- **Diversification:** is a risk management strategy that involves spreading investments across different assets, sectors, or geographical regions to reduce exposure to any single investment. The principle of diversification asserts that by holding a mix of uncorrelated investments, the overall risk of the portfolio is reduced. While some assets may underperform, others might outperform, helping to smooth out the overall performance of the portfolio.

- Diversification can be achieved across asset classes (e.g., stocks, bonds, real estate, commodities), industries, and geographical markets.
- This principle is based on the belief that "not putting all your eggs in one basket" helps protect against volatility.

- **Asset Allocation:** refers to the strategy of dividing a portfolio among different asset categories, such as equities, bonds, real estate, and cash. The goal of asset allocation is to balance risk and return in accordance with an investor's goals, risk tolerance, and investment time horizon. A well-thought-out asset allocation is crucial for achieving long-term investment success.
  - Strategic asset allocation involves a long-term allocation decision based on an investor's risk profile and financial objectives.
  - Tactical asset allocation allows for more short-term adjustments based on market conditions or changes in the investor's goals.
- **Compounding:** is the process by which the returns on an investment generate their own earnings. Over time, the interest or gains earned on an investment are reinvested, and this leads to the exponential growth of the initial investment. The power of compounding becomes particularly significant in long-term investments, where even modest returns can result in substantial growth.
  - The longer the investment horizon, the greater the effect of compounding.
  - Compounding can work for or against an investor, depending on whether the returns are positive or negative.
- **Liquidity:** refers to the ease with which an asset can be converted into cash without significant loss in value. Highly liquid assets, such as stocks and bonds, can be quickly sold and converted into cash, while less liquid

assets, such as real estate, may take longer to sell. The principle of liquidity is important for investors to consider, especially when they need to access their funds in emergencies or during market downturns.

- Liquidity risk is the risk that an investor will not be able to quickly sell an asset at a reasonable price, potentially forcing them to take a loss.
- Cash and government bonds are examples of highly liquid investments, while real estate and certain alternative investments may have lower liquidity.

- **Market Efficiency:** The principle of market efficiency suggests that financial markets reflect all available information at any given time, meaning that asset prices are always an accurate reflection of the true value of the underlying asset. According to the Efficient Market Hypothesis (EMH), it is impossible to consistently outperform the market through analysis or timing because all information is already incorporated into asset prices.
  - The EMH suggests that active management strategies are unlikely to beat the market in the long run, leading some investors to prefer passive investment strategies like index funds.
  - The efficiency of the market can vary depending on the type of market and the availability of information.
- **Capital Preservation:** focuses on safeguarding the initial investment amount. This principle is vital for conservative investors who prioritise protecting their capital over generating high returns. In such cases, investments with low risk and stable returns are preferred, even if they offer lower potential profits.
  - Common capital preservation investments include high-quality bonds, certificates of deposit, and money market funds.

- This principle is particularly relevant for individuals in retirement or those with short-term financial goals.

- **Investment Horizon** : The investment horizon refers to the length of time an investor expects to hold an investment before needing to access the funds. The investment horizon is closely tied to risk tolerance and the type of investments suitable for the investor. A long-term horizon typically allows for higher-risk investments, while a short-term horizon often requires more conservative choices.
  - Investors with a longer horizon can afford to take more risk because they have time to recover from potential losses.
  - Short-term investors, on the other hand, tend to focus on liquidity and stability, preferring low-risk investments.

1.6 Advantages and Risks of Financial Investment

This section explores the key benefits and potential drawbacks of financial investments, helping investors understand the trade-offs involved in building a diversified investment portfolio.

- **Advantages of Financial Investment**
  - **Capital Appreciation** : Financial investments have the potential to increase in value over time, especially in assets like stocks, real estate, or commodities. This capital appreciation can lead to substantial long-term gains for investors.
  - **Income Generation**: Investments such as bonds, dividend-paying stocks, and real estate can generate a steady stream of income. Investors may receive interest payments, dividends, or rental income, which can supplement their earnings.

- **Diversification**: By investing in a range of financial assets, investors can spread their risk. Diversification helps to reduce the impact of any single investment performing poorly, thereby stabilising overall portfolio performance.
- **Hedge Against Inflation**: Certain investments, such as real estate and commodities like gold, can act as hedges against inflation. They help preserve the purchasing power of invested capital during periods of rising prices.
- **Access to Growth Opportunities**: Financial investment opens up opportunities to participate in the growth of companies, sectors, or even entire economies. For example, investing in start-ups or emerging markets can lead to substantial returns if those companies or economies expand successfully.
- **Liquidity**: Some financial investments, like stocks and bonds, are highly liquid, meaning they can be quickly converted into cash if needed. This offers flexibility for investors to access funds in emergencies or take advantage of new investment opportunities.
- **Tax Benefits**: Some types of financial investments, such as retirement accounts or specific mutual funds, offer tax advantages. These may include tax deferrals or exemptions on income earned from the investments, helping to improve long-term returns.
- **Social and Environmental Impact Socially Responsible Investing (SRI)** or **Environmental, Social, and Governance (ESG)**: investing allows investors to support companies or projects that align with ethical, environmental, or social values. This provides investors with the opportunity to contribute positively to society while earning financial returns.

- **Risks of Financial Investment**

- **Market Volatility:** Financial markets are inherently volatile, with prices of stocks, bonds, and commodities often fluctuating based on economic conditions, political events, and market sentiment. This volatility can lead to potential losses, particularly in the short term.
- **Risk of Loss:** All investments carry a risk of loss, whether from market downturns, poor company performance, or other factors. In some cases, investors may lose a portion or all of their invested capital, especially in high-risk investments.
- **Interest Rate Risk**: Changes in interest rates can impact the value of financial investments. For example, bond prices typically fall when interest rates rise, as newly issued bonds offer higher returns. This can lead to losses for investors holding existing bonds.
- **Liquidity Risk**: Not all financial investments are easily liquidated. Real estate and certain alternative investments, such as private equity or collectibles, may be difficult to sell quickly without incurring significant losses, especially in a down market.
- **Inflation Risk**: While certain investments act as hedges against inflation, others, such as fixed-income securities, may be negatively impacted by rising inflation. This can erode the purchasing power of the returns from these investments over time.
- **Credit Risk**: When investing in bonds or other debt instruments, there is a risk that the issuer may default on its obligations. This is known as credit risk and can lead to a loss of principal and interest payments for the investor.
- **Transaction Costs and Fees:** Many financial investments involve transaction costs, such as broker

fees or management fees for mutual funds. These costs can diminish the overall return on investment, particularly for smaller or more frequent investments.

- **Dependence on Expertise**: Some types of financial investments, such as stocks or real estate, require a high level of expertise. Investors with limited knowledge may struggle to interpret market analyses or company performance, leading to poor investment decisions.
- **Behavioural Risks**: Financial markets are not always rational. Behavioural risks, such as panic selling during market downturns or overconfidence in bull markets, can lead to significant price fluctuations and losses for investors.
- **Legal and Regulatory Risks**: Unforeseen legal changes or government regulations can adversely affect certain investments, especially in sectors that are heavily regulated, such as energy, telecommunications, or healthcare.

Chapter Two
Introduction to Financial Markets

Chapter Two: Introduction to Financial Markets

Financial markets are a fundamental component of the modern economic structure, representing the platform through which money and financial resources are exchanged. These markets facilitate the flow of capital between individuals, businesses, and governments, providing essential means for investment and financing. In this chapter, we will explore the key concepts related to financial markets, including their definition, types, and significance in the contemporary economy. By understanding these fundamentals, the reader will gain a comprehensive insight into the role of financial markets in driving economic growth and ensuring financial stability.

2 .1 Definition of the Financial Market

A financial market is an organised platform or environment where individuals, companies, and institutions engage in the buying, selling, and trading of financial securities, commodities, and other fungible assets. These markets facilitate the efficient allocation of resources by connecting those who need capital (borrowers) with those who have surplus capital to invest (lenders). Financial markets can be physical spaces, like stock exchanges, or digital platforms operating globally.

At their core, financial markets exist to provide a structured mechanism for setting prices, enabling liquidity, reducing transaction costs, and transferring risk.

2.2 The Importance of Financial Markets

The importance of financial markets extends far beyond individual investors and companies:

- Economic Stability :Well-functioning financial markets contribute to the stability and resilience of the economy by efficiently allocating capital and managing risks.
- Wealth Creation: Markets offer investment opportunities that allow individuals and institutions to grow their wealth over time.
- Capital Formation: Financial markets help companies and governments raise necessary funds for expansion, infrastructure development, and innovation.
- International Integration: Global financial markets connect economies across borders, facilitating international trade, investment, and economic cooperation.
- Policy Implementation: Governments and central banks often rely on financial markets to implement monetary and fiscal policies through the issuance and trading of government securities.

2.3 Participants in the Financial Market

Participants in financial markets are typically classified into four major groups according to their roles: capital seekers, capital providers, intermediaries, and regulatory authorities. Each group plays a crucial role in maintaining the efficiency, liquidity, and stability of financial markets.
Below is a detailed categorisation of these participants:

- **Capital Seekers (Demanders of Funds)**
  Capital seekers are entities that require funding to finance investment projects, operations, or government spending. They enter financial markets to obtain funds by issuing financial instruments such as stocks, bonds, or other securities.

Types of Capital Seekers:

- Corporations: Issue shares or corporate bonds to raise funds for expansion, research and development, or operations.
- Governments and Municipalities: Issue sovereign bonds or municipal bonds to finance infrastructure projects, budget deficits, or public services.
- Entrepreneurs and Start-ups: Seek capital through venture capitalists, angel investors, or initial public offerings (IPOs).
- Financial Institutions: Sometimes seek funding by issuing debt instruments or through interbank lending.

• **Capital Providers** (Suppliers of Funds)

Capital providers supply the necessary funds in financial markets, investing their surplus capital to achieve returns or preserve wealth.

Types of Capital Providers:

- Individual Investors: Private individuals investing in securities, mutual funds, real estate, or pension plans.
- Institutional Investors: Large entities like pension funds, insurance companies, mutual funds, sovereign wealth funds, and hedge funds.
- Banks and Financial Institutions: Provide loans, purchase securities, or invest surplus liquidity in various financial instruments.

• **Financial Intermediaries**: Financial intermediaries facilitate the flow of funds between capital seekers and providers. They create efficient markets by reducing transaction costs, spreading risk, and providing valuable services such as underwriting, advisory, and market-making.

Types of Financial Intermediaries:

- Banks: Offer deposit accounts, loans, and investment services.

- Investment Banks: Specialise in underwriting new securities, facilitating mergers and acquisitions, and corporate advisory services.
- Brokers and Dealers: Brokers act as agents executing trades for clients, while dealers trade on their own account.
- Asset Management Companies: Manage collective investments such as mutual funds, ETFs, and private equity funds.
- Insurance Companies: Invest premium income to generate returns, providing liquidity and risk management solutions.

- **Regulatory Authorities** : Regulatory bodies ensure that financial markets operate fairly, transparently, and efficiently. They protect investors, maintain market integrity, and minimise systemic risks.
  Types of Regulatory Authorities:
  - Central Banks: Such as the Bank of England, which regulates monetary policy, manages inflation, and supervises major financial institutions.
  - Financial Regulatory Agencies: Entities like the Financial Conduct Authority (FCA) in the UK, or the Securities and Exchange Commission (SEC) in the US, oversee market activities, enforce compliance, and protect investors.
  - International Regulatory Organisations: Institutions like the Basel Committee on Banking Supervision and the International Organisation of Securities Commissions (IOSCO) set global standards for financial regulation.

2.4 Functions of the Capital Market

Financial markets serve a range of critical functions within the global economy. They facilitate the efficient allocation of resources, promote economic growth, and provide mechanisms for managing risk and liquidity. Understanding these functions is essential for comprehending the broader role of financial systems in supporting business activity, innovation, and government operations.

This section discusses the principal functions of financial markets, supported by academic insights.

- **Mobilisation and Allocation of Savings:** Financial markets act as intermediaries, mobilising individual and institutional savings and channelling them towards productive investment opportunities. This process ensures that surplus funds are directed where they can generate the highest economic returns, contributing to capital formation and economic development.
  - Households deposit savings into banks or invest in securities.
  - Firms and governments access these funds to finance business ventures and public infrastructure.
- **Facilitation of Price Discovery:** A key function of financial markets is to determine the price of financial instruments through the forces of supply and demand. Financial markets collect and aggregate information about the value of assets, and through continuous trading, set prices that reflect the consensus valuation among market participants
  - Transparent pricing enables investors to make informed decisions.
  - Accurate price discovery helps resources flow to their most efficient uses.
- **Provision of Liquidity:** Financial markets provide liquidity, allowing investors to buy and sell assets with relative ease. Liquid markets enable participants to quickly convert their investments into cash without causing significant price distortions

- High liquidity reduces the risk associated with holding assets.
- It encourages more participation by both individual and institutional investors.

- **Risk Management and Diversification:** Through financial instruments such as derivatives, insurance contracts, and diversified portfolios, financial markets allow participants to manage and transfer risk. Investors can hedge against adverse price movements or diversify their investments to reduce unsystematic risk
  - Risk-sharing enhances economic stability.
  - Derivatives like options and futures allow investors to lock in prices or insure against volatility.
- **Reduction of Transaction Costs:** Financial markets reduce the costs associated with exchanging assets by providing centralised mechanisms for trading. Standardised contracts, transparent regulations, and competitive brokerages minimise the time, effort, and money needed to buy or sell securities.
  - Lower transaction costs encourage greater trading activity.
  - They also increase overall market efficiency and accessibility.
- **Promotion of Economic Growth :** By efficiently allocating resources and encouraging investment, financial markets stimulate economic growth. Firms can fund research and development, governments can finance infrastructure, and individuals can build wealth, all of which contribute to improving living standards
  - A strong financial market ecosystem is closely associated with innovation and productivity.
  - Emerging markets particularly benefit from well-functioning financial systems.

- **Enhancement of Financial Stability:** Financial markets help stabilise the economy by distributing risks more evenly across participants and sectors. Well-regulated markets can absorb shocks more effectively, reducing the likelihood of systemic crises.
  - Mechanisms like circuit breakers and reserve requirements enhance resilience.
  - Regulatory oversight ensures that speculative excesses are minimised.

2.5 Structure of the Financial Market

The financial market is not a homogeneous entity; rather, it is composed of distinct sectors, each serving specific functions and participants. These sectors are differentiated based on the nature of the instruments traded, the duration of the investment, the method of trading, and the purpose of transactions. Below is a deeper classification:

- **Based on the Nature of the Instrument**
  - **Capital Markets :** Capital markets deal with financial instruments intended for long-term financing, typically exceeding one year. They facilitate the raising of capital for governments, corporations, and institutions.
    - Equity Markets: Where ownership securities such as shares are issued and traded.
    - Debt Markets: Where debt instruments like corporate bonds and government bonds are traded.

- **Money Markets:** Money markets handle short-term debt instruments, usually with maturities less than one year. These markets are critical for maintaining liquidity within the financial system, Facilitating short-term borrowing and lending, managing liquidity needs, and ensuring financial system stability. Examples: Treasury bills, commercial papers, certificates of deposit, repurchase agreements.

- **Based on the Stage of Security Trading**
  - **Primary Markets:** The primary market is where new financial instruments are created and offered for the first time. It enables entities to raise fresh capital.
    Example:Companies issuing shares through an Initial Public Offering (IPO).
    Key Feature: Investors purchase securities directly from the issuer.
  - **Secondary Markets:** The secondary market involves the trading of previously issued securities among investors. No new capital is raised for the issuer.
    Examples: Stock exchanges such as the London Stock Exchange or the NASDAQ.
    Key Feature: Provides liquidity, allowing investors to easily enter or exit investments.
- **Based on Trading Mechanism**
  - **Organised (Exchange-Based) Markets:** In these markets, trading occurs on regulated platforms where rules ensure transparency and fairness.
    Examples: London Stock Exchange, New York Stock Exchange.
    Advantages:
    High liquidity, reduced counterparty risk, transparent pricing.
  - **Over-the-Counter (OTC) Markets:** OTC markets involve direct trading between parties without a centralised exchange. They are less regulated and offer customised contracts.
    Examples: Currency markets (Forex), some types of bond and derivatives markets.
    Advantages: Flexibility in contract terms; however, they come with higher counterparty risk.

- **Based on the Type of Product**
  - **Derivatives Markets:** Derivatives markets deal with instruments whose value is derived from underlying assets such as commodities, interest rates, or currencies.
    Products: Futures, options, swaps, forwards.
    Purpose: Risk management (hedging), speculation, and arbitrage opportunities.
  - **Foreign Exchange (Forex) Markets:** Forex markets facilitate the trading of currencies between participants globally, supporting international trade and investment.
    Features: Decentralised, highly liquid, operates 24 hours a day.
  - **Commodity Markets** Commodity markets are concerned with the trading of raw materials and primary products.
    Examples: Gold, oil, agricultural products.
    Purpose: Price discovery, risk management, and speculation.

Chapter Three Financial Market Instruments

Chapter Three: Financial Market Instruments

Financial markets are a dynamic platform that allows the exchange of funds and securities, playing a pivotal role in the global economy. These markets encompass various instruments that enable participants—ranging from individual investors to large corporations and governments—to manage their capital, hedge risks, and optimise returns. This chapter delves into the core financial instruments that define these markets, including those in the money and capital markets, as well as complex derivatives.

3.1 The money market

The money market constitutes the first segment of the broader financial market. It represents the platform for the trading of short-term financial assets, primarily aimed at facilitating financial transactions between units experiencing a temporary financial deficit and those possessing a temporary financial surplus. This is achieved through the exchange of short-term instruments.

The primary function of the money market is to ensure efficient liquidity management, bridging the gap between borrowers and lenders in the short term. Key institutions operating within the money market include the central bank, commercial banks, as well as other financial entities such as investment banks and postal savings funds involved in short-term deposit and lending operations.

- **Key Characteristics of the Money Market**

The fundamental characteristics of the money market can be summarised as follows:

- High security levels: Most money market instruments are highly secure and are often used as collateral for loans.

- Attractive returns: The market offers a suitable return for investors who prefer low-risk investments and wish to avoid significant exposure to financial uncertainty.
- In the money market, short-term financial instruments are traded, with maturity periods typically ranging from one day to one year.
- The money market is characterised by high liquidity, as most of the instruments traded within it possess high marketability, meaning they can be quickly converted into cash with minimal price distortion.

- **Segmentation of the Money Market**

The money market itself is divided into two main segments:

- **Primary Money Market:** The primary money market is where new short-term financial instruments are issued. It facilitates the raising of funds for short-term employment, with interest rates determined according to the source of funds, the borrower's financial standing, and their creditworthiness.
- **Secondary Money Market:** The secondary money market is where existing short-term financial instruments are traded. Prices in this market are determined by the fundamental forces of supply and demand.

The secondary market is subdivided into two main segments based on the type of operations conducted:

- Discount Market: The discount market involves the discounting of short-term credit instruments, such as: Commercial papers, Bankers' acceptances, Treasury bills
- Short-Term Loan Market: This market includes all types of short-term loans, typically ranging from one week to one year. It is mainly composed of transactions between:

- o Enterprises and individuals (seeking short-term financing)
- o Commercial banks and specialised lending institutions offering short-term credit facilities.

3.2 Money Market Instruments

There are several instruments in the money market, including the following:

- **Treasury Bills** :Treasury bills are government-issued securities designed to provide funds needed to finance short-term activities, typically with maturities of less than one year. They are characterised by ease of liquidation without exposing the holder to capital losses, high liquidity, and the absence of credit risk. Holders of treasury bills do not receive interest; instead, their return is the difference between the purchase price and the face value paid upon maturity. If sold before maturity, the return is the difference between the selling price and the purchase price.
- **Commercial Papers**: A commercial paper is a short-term debt instrument issued by well-known companies or those with high creditworthiness to meet short-term funding needs without requiring collateral. The issuer of the paper pays its value to the holder upon maturity. These papers are sold at a discount from their face value, and the obligation of commercial banks to honour these papers minimises the risk of investment in them. However, this risk remains slightly higher than that of treasury bills.
- **Bankers' Acceptances**: This instrument is among the oldest in the money market, originally created to facilitate international trade. It is a written commitment to repay a loan borrowed by an individual from a bank. The bank may hold this acceptance until maturity or sell it to another party, who may then sell it to a third party, and so on. At

maturity, the holder of the acceptance is entitled to recover its value from the original borrower. If the borrower fails to pay, the holder can seek repayment from the bank that initially accepted the commitment.

- **Negotiable Certificates of Deposit**: These certificates are receipts issued by banks, confirming that the holder has deposited a specific sum for a fixed period at a predetermined interest rate. Holders can sell or transfer the certificate or wait until its maturity date. Since these certificates represent time deposits, they cannot be redeemed before maturity from the issuing bank. The only way to liquidate them before the maturity date is by selling them in the secondary market.
- **Eurodollar Loans**: The term "Eurodollar" refers to US dollars deposited in banks outside the United States, particularly European banks. The Eurodollar market comprises large banks that deal exclusively in dollars, accepting deposits and granting loans in US dollars. These loans are notable for their large size and short maturity periods. Eurodollars accumulate in European banks when banks or companies withdraw deposits from US banks and redeposit them as term deposits in European banks, often due to higher interest rates or regulatory restrictions imposed on US banks.
- **Repurchase Agreements (Repos)**: Repurchase agreements are a borrowing method used by traders specialising in buying and selling securities to convert an additional stock of marketable securities into cash for one night or a few days, sometimes extending up to a month or more. In these agreements, traders approach specialised brokers to arrange a deal with an investor seeking an opportunity to lend excess funds. Under the agreement, the trader temporarily sells securities equivalent to the amount needed and simultaneously agrees to repurchase them at a

slightly higher price on a specified date. The difference between the sale price and the repurchase price represents the interest on the borrowed funds. It is worth noting that the sale does not transfer possession of the securities to the investor, as the securities remain with the trader but are considered collateral for the investor under the agreement.

- **Federal Funds**: Also known as surplus reserve loans, these are funds that banks with surplus reserves lend to banks facing reserve shortages. These loans are based on an unwritten but guaranteed commitment from the central bank. The borrowing bank agrees to repay the loan along with the agreed interest. Federal funds are typically overnight loans intended to cover shortfalls in mandatory reserve requirements.
- **Call Money** refers to extremely short-term loans that can be recalled by the lender at any time without prior notice. These loans are often utilised between banks and financial institutions to manage daily liquidity requirements. Due to their very short maturity periods, often lasting only a day or less, interest rates for call money are highly sensitive to market conditions.
- **Bank Drafts** are payment instruments issued by banks on behalf of their clients and serve as guarantees for commercial transactions. These drafts are commonly used in both domestic and international trade, particularly in large-scale transactions. Their primary advantage lies in offering a secure method of payment, ensuring the completion of commercial agreements.
- **Money Market Mutual Funds** are collective investment schemes that pool funds from multiple investors to invest in short-term money market instruments such as treasury bills and certificates of deposit. These funds are designed to provide stable returns while maintaining high liquidity. They are particularly appealing to investors seeking a

secure and low-risk investment option with immediate accessibility to their funds.

- **Interbank Loans** are short-term loans exchanged between banks to address temporary liquidity shortages. These loans, which are typically unsecured, help banks meet reserve requirements or other financial obligations. The interest rates for interbank loans are determined by market conditions, and the loans are a key component of the interbank money market.
- **Banker's Drafts** resemble cheques but are fully guaranteed by the issuing bank. These instruments are frequently used in commercial transactions or to settle obligations between parties. Banker's drafts are particularly favoured in international trade due to their higher level of security compared to personal cheques.
- **Treasury Notes** are short- to medium-term debt instruments issued by governments to fund short-term deficits. While primarily designed for short-term use, some treasury notes have maturities extending up to two years, making them a hybrid instrument between short- and medium-term investments. They are highly liquid and often traded in secondary markets.
- **Foreign Exchange Swaps** are agreements between two parties to exchange currencies for a short-term period and reverse the exchange at a pre-agreed rate at a later date. These swaps are widely used in international markets to address short-term currency liquidity needs or to hedge against exchange rate fluctuations. Their flexibility makes them a popular tool in managing foreign exchange risks.
- **Short-Term Municipal Notes** are bonds issued by local governments or municipalities to fund infrastructure projects or cover operational expenses. These instruments are particularly attractive to investors looking for short-term investments with potential tax advantages. Their

short maturities, typically less than one year, make them highly liquid and relatively low-risk.

- **Floating Rate Notes** are short-term debt instruments with variable interest rates that adjust periodically based on market rates. These notes are popular among institutional investors as they provide protection against interest rate fluctuations while offering stable returns. Their maturities generally range from short to medium term, depending on the issuer's needs.
- **Certificates of Deposit (Fixed-Term)** are traditional time deposits issued by banks for a fixed period at a predetermined interest rate. Unlike negotiable certificates of deposit, these instruments cannot be traded in secondary markets. Investors must hold them until maturity to redeem their value, making them suitable for those seeking stable and predictable returns.

Below is a table categorising the money market instruments based on their tradability in exchanges (e.g., stock exchanges) versus their trade in over-the-counter (OTC) or secondary markets:

Money Market Instrument	Tradability on Exchanges	Tradability in OTC/Secondary Markets
Treasury Bills	Rarely traded on exchanges; some jurisdictions may allow it.	Frequently traded in OTC or secondary money markets.
Commercial Papers	Not traded on exchanges.	Primarily traded in OTC markets between institutional investors.

Bankers' Acceptances	Not traded on exchanges.	Commonly traded in OTC and secondary markets.
Negotiable Certificates of Deposit	Occasionally traded on exchanges (depending on regulations).	Commonly traded in secondary markets.
Eurodollar Loans	Not traded on exchanges.	Traded privately between banks and financial institutions.
Repurchase Agreements (Repos)	Not traded on exchanges.	Exclusively traded in OTC markets between specialised traders.
Federal Funds	Not traded on exchanges.	Traded directly between banks through the Federal Funds market.
Call Money	Not traded on exchanges.	Traded directly between financial institutions.
Bank Drafts	Rarely traded on exchanges.	Typically used in OTC or direct institutional transactions.
Money Market Mutual Funds	Not traded on exchanges.	Traded indirectly through fund issuers.
Interbank Loans	Not traded on exchanges.	Conducted directly between banks in OTC settings.
Floating Rate Notes	Occasionally traded on exchanges.	Frequently traded in OTC markets.
Short-Term Municipal Notes	Rarely traded on exchanges.	Commonly traded in OTC markets.

Foreign Exchange Swaps	Not traded on exchanges.	Exclusively traded in OTC and private international markets

3.3 Capital Market

The capital market represents the space where the forces of supply and demand meet. It is the marketplace where economic entities with temporary financial deficits and surpluses trade capital, such as securities, medium- and long-term loans, and other financial instruments. The primary function of the capital market is to provide a structured platform for transactions in these financial assets.

- **Segments of the Capital Market**

The capital market is divided into two main segments:

- **Medium and Long-Term Loan Market** : This segment of the capital market is dedicated to providing loans with repayment periods exceeding one year. It involves institutions like mortgage banks and industrial development banks offering long-term funding solutions to enterprises and other borrowers.

- **Securities Market** : The securities market is further divided into two main categories based on the role they serve:

    - **Primary Market**: The primary market is where new issues of financial instruments are offered to the public for the first time. It represents the direct relationship between the issuer of the securities and the investors. This market is often referred to as the wholesale market, where securities are sold in bulk to the public. The main role of financial intermediaries, such as investment banks and commercial banks, is crucial in marketing these securities or committing to marketing them for a commission. The primary objective of this market is to raise funds for establishing new projects or expanding existing ones to increase their capital.

In the primary market, the financial intermediaries' responsibilities include:

- Advising on the volume and timing of the issue.
- Executing the issue, including all necessary procedures and public relations.
- Committing to distributing the entire issue or a minimum agreed-upon amount, often for a fee.

- **Secondary Market:** Also known as the trading market, the secondary market provides the flexibility for investors to trade financial securities at mutually agreed-upon prices between buyers and sellers. This feature is known as market continuity, ensuring there is always a buyer and seller available for securities. The secondary market enables liquidity, where securities can be converted into cash before their maturity dates, providing flexibility for investors. Crucially, the proceeds from the transactions in this market go directly to investors, not to the companies that initially issued the securities.

  The secondary market is divided into organized and unorganized segments:

- Organized Market (Stock Exchange): This is where financial instruments listed for regular trading according to specific rules are exchanged. The organized market operates under a well-regulated environment, managed by a market or exchange committee composed of elected members from registered companies, brokers, and government representatives. Their duties include managing and regulating securities trading, overseeing the listing process, monitoring violations, and allocating trading platforms. Examples of organized markets include the New York Stock Exchange and the London Stock Exchange.

The key benefits of listing securities in the organized market are:

- ✓ Free Advertising: Listing is a free way of advertising the security, with its effectiveness increasing as trading activity rises.
- ✓ Improved Credit Image: Listing enhances the credibility and financial standing of the issuing company, making it easier to obtain cheaper financing.
- ✓ Investor Access to Information: Investors can obtain relevant information about the company and the securities being offered, facilitating their decision-making process.
- ✓ Protection Against Fraud: Listing provides a safeguard against fraud and misleading transactions, ensuring that all dealings in the market are transparent and legitimate.

- ▪ Unorganized Market (Over-the-Counter - OTC): The OTC market operates outside traditional exchanges and facilitates transactions through brokers or dealers. It is a decentralized market where securities are traded without the centralized oversight seen in organized exchanges. The OTC market is managed by a network of traders who are connected through robust communication systems, enabling them to determine the best prices. These traders are referred to as market makers. A well-known example of this market is the NASDAQ, which operates under the National Association of Securities Dealers Automated Quotations (NASDAQ).

The OTC market is subdivided into two main segments:

- ✓ **Third Market**: This market involves transactions where securities listed on exchanges are traded outside of them. Institutional investors, like pension funds, participate in this market, often to negotiate lower commission rates.
- ✓ **Fourth Market**: The fourth market involves direct transactions between large institutions without the need for brokers or dealers. This segment reduces the costs associated with intermediary fees and allows for faster, more efficient trades through electronic communication networks (ECNs).

- Key Benefits of the Secondary Market:

- Liquidity: The secondary market ensures the continuous liquidity of securities, allowing investors to buy and sell their holdings before the securities reach maturity.
- Market Efficiency: It enhances the efficiency of the primary market by enabling price discovery and providing investors with the flexibility to exit investments whenever required.

3.3 Capital Market Instruments

Capital market instruments are essential tools for raising long-term funds, enabling both issuers and investors to participate in the growth and development of businesses and economies through a variety of financial instruments such as equities, bonds, and hybrids.

3.4.1 Shares

Shares represent an ownership instrument in a public joint-stock company. They are uniform-value certificates that can be traded in stock exchanges through commercial methods. Shares signify a participant's stake in the capital of a company, which consists of monetary or in-kind contributions.

From an investor's perspective, shares can hold various types of values:

- **Issued Value (Nominal Value):** The value specified in the incorporation contract, issued in the primary market during subscription.
- **Book Value (Accounting Value):** Determined by the balance sheet, it is calculated by dividing shareholders' equity (including retained earnings, reserves, and profits) by the total number of declared and subscribed shares.
- **Market Value (Traded Value):** The value at which the share is traded in the secondary market, representing the shareholder's current wealth in the market.
- **Fair Value:** This is derived by dividing expected cash flows by the required rate of return. It reflects the share's potential to generate future cash flows.
- **Liquidation Value:** The cash flow received by a shareholder when a company ceases operations and undergoes liquidation.

- **Types of Shares**

a) Based on Form:

- Registered Shares: Issued in the name of the shareholder, and transferring ownership requires returning to the issuer or stock exchange.
- Order Shares: The shareholder's identity is not known to the company, and ownership is transferred through endorsement.
- Bearer Shares: Not issued in the name of any individual and ownership transfers simply by handing over the share certificate to another party.

b) Based on Original Contributions:

- In-Kind Shares: Represent contributions in kind, such as real estate or machinery, as part of the company's capital.
- Cash Shares: Issued in exchange for monetary contributions.

c) Based on Capital Structure:

- Authorised Shares: The amount of capital authorised by the company's founding documents, divided into equal parts called authorised shares.
- Issued Shares: The portion of authorised capital covered by actual issued shares.
- Treasury Shares: Issued shares that are reacquired by the company or donated back by shareholders.
- Outstanding Shares: The remaining shares in circulation after deducting the repurchased shares from the issued shares.
- Paid-Up Shares: Shares for which the full value has been paid. If not fully paid upon subscription, they are called partially paid shares. Shares distributed for free as compensation for unrealised distributions are referred to as unpaid shares.

d) Based on Rights:

- Common Shares: Entitle holders to regular dividends, voting rights, participation in the general assembly, and a share in the company's assets upon liquidation. Ownership transfer does not require prior approval from the company.
- Preferred Shares: Offer additional rights compared to common shares, such as priority in receiving fixed dividends, priority in liquidation proceeds after bondholders, cumulative dividend rights, and the ability to convert into common shares.

e) **Based on Redeemability (Repayment of Value):**
   - Capital Shares: These shares are not redeemable during the company's existence and remain part of the company's capital.
   - Enjoyment Shares: Issued to replace redeemed shares during the company's operations. Holders have similar rights as capital shares except for lower profit entitlements.

F) Emerging Trends in Common Shares
   - **Common Shares for Specific Production Divisions:** Distributions are linked to the production volume or profitability of a particular division.
   - **Tax-Deductible Common Shares:** Dividends are deducted from revenue before tax calculation.
   - **Guaranteed Common Shares:** Provide holders with the right to claim compensation from the issuing company if the market price of the shares decreases within a specified period.

Notes on Redeemable Shares
   - **Capital Shares:** Retain their value without repayment during the company's lifecycle.
   - **Enjoyment Shares:** Issued to compensate partners for redeemed shares, granting similar rights to capital shares but lower profit entitlements.

Advantages and Disadvantages of Equity Financing" Shares" from the Issuing Institution's Perspective

Advantages of Equity Financing

a) **No Fixed Obligations:** Common shares do not impose fixed obligations on the issuing institution. Dividend distribution to shareholders occurs only after the company generates profits and decides to distribute them.

b) **No Maturity Date:**Common shares do not have a specified maturity date, providing long-term flexibility to the issuing company.
c) **Reduction in Debt Ratio:** Issuing additional common shares reduces the proportion of borrowed funds in the capital structure. This, in turn, increases the institution's borrowing capacity when needed, assuming other factors remain constant.
d) **No Repayment Obligation:**The institution is not required to repay the value of common shares on a specific date, granting flexibility and eliminating the need for predetermined financial commitments

Disadvantages of Equity Financing

a) **Dilution of Ownership:** Issuing common shares introduces new shareholders and expands the ownership base. This increases the number of individuals with voting rights, decision-making power, and oversight over the institution. If the new shareholders acquire a significant portion of the capital, it may lead to changes in the company's management approach to align with their preferences.
b) **Reduced Earnings Per Share (EPS):** Expanding the shareholder base results in a reduction in EPS for existing investors. Additionally, new shareholders share in retained earnings or previously realised profits, as well as future profits, reducing the returns for earlier investors.
c) **Higher Cost of Capital:** Issuing common shares increases the cost of capital for two reasons:
   - **Higher Risk:** The risk associated with investing in common shares is higher than that of other financial instruments, leading investors to demand higher returns.

- **No Tax Savings:** Unlike bond interest, dividends on common shares are not tax-deductible. As a result, the issuing company does not benefit from tax savings, further raising the effective cost of equity financing.

3.4.2 Preferred Shares

Preferred shares are a type of long-term financial instrument that companies issue to finance their needs. These shares are often used by companies to attract investors to subscribe and contribute to expanding their capital and funding new projects. Preferred shares have nominal value, book value, and market value.

The market value and nominal value are similar to those of common shares. However, the book value of preferred shares is calculated as the value recorded in the company's accounts divided by the total number of issued shares.

Preferred shares are similar to common shares in representing an equity stake in the company, and shareholders are entitled to claim dividends when profits are distributed. However, they resemble bonds in offering fixed returns based on a percentage of the nominal value. Preferred shareholders do not have voting rights, but they have priority over common shareholders in receiving dividends and claims during liquidation.

- **Characteristics of Preferred Shares**

Each characteristic is associated with a specific type of preferred share:

- **Cumulative Dividends:** Preferred shares often have cumulative dividend rights, where unpaid dividends accumulate over time and are paid out later. This right is typically not available to common shareholders and applies to cumulative preferred shares.
- **Convertible Shares:** Preferred shares may be convertible into common shares. This conversion is

often chosen when holders observe higher dividend distributions for common shares compared to their fixed returns.

  - **Callable Shares:** Companies issuing callable preferred shares have the right to redeem these shares by purchasing them back from holders or exchanging them for common shares, depending on the company's preferences.

- **New Trends in Preferred Shares**
  - **Variable Distribution Preferred Shares:** Introduced in the United States in 1982, these shares tie their dividends to the yield of Treasury bonds. Dividend payouts are adjusted quarterly based on changes in Treasury bond yields, typically within a range of 7.5% to 15.5% of the nominal value of the share.
  - **Voting Rights for Preferred Shares:** Some preferred shares are issued with voting rights to compensate common shareholders for a decline in the market value of their shares.
- **Advantages and Disadvantages of Financing with Preferred Shares from the Issuing Institution's Perspective**
  - **Advantages:**
    - **No Obligation to Pay Dividends Annually:** The company is not legally required to distribute dividends every year it earns profits. When dividends are paid, they are limited to a fixed percentage of the nominal value.
    - **No Participation in Management:** Preferred shares often include provisions preventing holders from participating in company management, board elections, or voting at general assemblies. This allows the company to retain full control over its

operations without the risk of losing control to shareholders.

  - **Reduction in Debt Ratio:** Issuing preferred shares decreases the company's reliance on borrowed funds, thereby increasing its future borrowing capacity.
  - **No Maturity Date:** Preferred shares do not have a fixed maturity date, eliminating the need to create reserves for repayment.
- **Disadvantages**
  - **Taxable Dividends:** Dividends on preferred shares are subject to taxation, offering no tax savings to the issuing company, unlike bond interest payments.
  - **Cumulative Dividend Obligation:** Preferred shareholders are entitled to receive their dividends before common shareholders. If the company does not declare dividends in a given year, these dividends accumulate and must be paid when distributions resume. This cumulative nature can impose a financial burden on the company.

3.4.3 Bonds

Bonds are debt instruments and a source of borrowed financing that companies and governments use to meet large financial needs that cannot be funded by a single entity. The required amount is divided into smaller denominations and issued to the public.

A bond is a financial security that represents a debt and can be issued by a company or government. It is essentially a written promise by the borrower (issuer) to pay a specific amount of money (nominal value) to the bondholder on a specified date, along with periodic interest payments on the nominal value.

- **Characteristics of Bonds**
  - **Nominal Value:** This is the value at which the bond is issued initially, and it remains fixed from the issuance date until the maturity or repayment date. Bonds also have a current value, which represents the price at which the bond is traded in financial markets (secondary markets).
  - **Interest Rate:** The interest, also called the coupon, is the compensation the borrower pays to the lender for using the funds over a specified period. The bondholder receives this fixed interest regardless of whether the company earns a profit or not.
  - **Maturity Date:** This is the agreed-upon date on which the bond's principal amount is repaid to investors. Bonds typically have relatively long maturities, and the issuer cannot demand early repayment. In the event of company liquidation, bondholders have priority over shareholders in receiving their dues, equivalent to the bond's nominal value.
  - **No Participation in Management:** Bondholders do not have voting rights or the ability to participate in shareholders' general assemblies.
  - Issuing bonds requires a resolution from the company's general assembly of shareholders to approve a public subscription, typically facilitated by a bank or a non-banking financial institution.
- **Types of Bonds**

a) Based on the Issuing Entity:

- **Public Bonds:** Issued by governments to meet borrowing needs, typically through the treasury or public institutions.

- **Private Bonds:** Issued by companies when they require external financing or liquidity for project expansion.

b) **Based on Security:**
   - **Secured Bonds:** These bonds are backed by specific assets such as land, buildings, or equipment. If the issuing company is unable to meet its obligations or liquidates, bondholders can claim the collateral assets to recover their investment.
   - **Unsecured Bonds:** These bonds are not backed by specific assets. The primary guarantee for bondholders is the issuing company's total assets and financial position.

c) **Based on Transferability and Ownership:**
   - **Registered Bonds:** The issuer retains the right to record the name of the current bondholder on the bond certificate. Ownership transfer requires approval from the issuer and must be recorded in the company's books following legal rules. Registered bonds can be fully registered, covering both principal and interest, or partially registered, where only the principal is registered, and interest is claimed using attached coupons.
   - **Bearer Bonds:**
     These bonds do not bear the bondholder's name and are transferred through physical delivery. Coupons attached to the bond are used to claim interest payments directly from the designated authority upon maturity.

d) **Based on Callable or Non-Callable Features:**
   - **Non-Callable Bonds:** These bonds allow the holder to retain them until maturity. The issuer cannot recall or redeem these bonds before the agreed maturity date unless specified in the issuance contract.

- **Callable Bonds:** These bonds include a call provision, allowing the issuer to redeem them before maturity. Callable bonds are often issued with a call premium to encourage investors to purchase them, as the call provision can be exploited by the issuer to the detriment of the investor when market conditions are favourable.

e) **Based on Convertibility:**
   - **Convertible Bonds:** These bonds come with an explicit provision in the issuance contract, allowing the bondholder to convert them into common shares at a predetermined price within a specific period.
   - **Non-Convertible Bonds:** The default type of bonds, which cannot be converted into shares. These bonds typically offer higher interest rates compared to convertible bonds.

f) **Based on Interest Rate:**
   - **Fixed-Rate Bonds:** These bonds have a fixed interest rate specified in the issuance contract, which remains unchanged throughout the bond's term.
   - **Floating-Rate Bonds:** These bonds have interest rates that fluctuate in line with prevailing market rates, often linked to a benchmark such as LIBOR.

g) **Emerging Trends in Bonds**
   - **Floating-Rate Bonds:** Introduced in the early 1980s to address inflationary pressures that increased interest rates, reducing bond market values. These bonds have an initial interest rate that is adjusted periodically, typically every six months, to align with prevailing market rates.
   - **Zero-Coupon Bonds:** Sold at a discount to their nominal value, these bonds do not pay periodic interest. The investor receives the nominal value at maturity, with the difference between the purchase price and nominal value representing the return.

- **Income Bonds:** Unlike traditional bonds, income bonds tie interest payments to the issuing company's profitability. If the company does not generate sufficient profits in a given year, bondholders cannot claim interest payments. Some issuance contracts, however, may allow unpaid interest to be carried forward and paid from future profits.
- **Junk Bonds:** Emerging in the 1980s, these high-risk bonds were issued to finance significant acquisitions by company board members, enabling them to purchase a substantial share of the company's publicly traded stock.

- **Bond Repayment Methods**
  - **Repayment at Maturity:** The company repays the bond's nominal value to the bondholder upon reaching the maturity date. This method allows the company to utilise the entire loan amount for the bond's duration, only paying annual interest during the term.
  - **Amortised Repayment:** The repayment is made in instalments over the loan term. Each year, a predetermined portion of the bonds is selected by lottery for repayment.
  - **Early Repayment:** Bonds can be repaid before the maturity date only if explicitly stated in the issuance contract.
- **Advantages and Disadvantages of Bond Financing**
  - **Advantages:**
    - Provides access to substantial funds at a cost lower than the expected return on investment.
    - Allows the company to utilise external funds without granting the lenders participation rights in management, ensuring operational flexibility.

    - Offers financial structure management flexibility by including provisions for recalling or extinguishing bonds when needed.
- **Disadvantages:**
    - Fixed bond costs become burdensome if the company faces financial difficulties.
    - Bonds typically have a fixed maturity date, requiring the company to create reserves for repayment or issue new bonds to refinance existing ones.
    - Financial difficulties can lead to prioritising bondholder payments over shareholder returns, reducing earnings per share and potentially lowering the company's market value in secondary markets.

3.4.4 Derivatives

Derivatives are financial contracts whose value is derived from the underlying financial assets, such as bonds and stocks. These contracts are secondary instruments built on primary investment contracts. Derivatives are used in financial markets for hedging, speculation, and arbitrage purposes.

The broad variety of derivatives and their differences make it challenging to define them precisely. The main types of derivatives include:

3.4.4.1 Futures Contracts

Futures contracts give the holder the right to buy or sell a specified quantity of an asset at a predetermined price, with the delivery and payment occurring on a future date. These contracts are standardised and traded on organised exchanges, covering a variety of assets, including commodities, financial instruments, and foreign currencies.

- **Types of Financial Futures Contracts**

Financial futures refer to contracts on original financial instruments. They include:

A. **Futures on Stocks:** Although there are no actual futures contracts on individual stocks in practice, they are theoretically possible and practically implementable.
B. **Futures on Fixed-Income Securities:** These are known as interest rate futures and involve securities with fixed income.
C. **Futures on Stock Indices:** A stock index represents the movement of stock prices in the market and is calculated based on a representative sample of traded stocks.
   - Futures on stock indices involve a contractual agreement between two parties where one agrees to pay the other the difference between the index value on a specific date (delivery date) and the agreed price (strike price).
   - If the index value exceeds the strike price, the seller pays the difference to the buyer, and vice versa.
   - The difference is usually multiplied by a fixed multiplier unique to each index.
   - Positions can be closed prior to the delivery date by entering into an opposite transaction (e.g., selling if the initial position was a buy and vice versa).

3.4.4.2 Options Contracts

An options contract grants the holder the right, but not the obligation, to buy or sell a financial instrument at a specific price (strike price) on or before a specified date. The buyer pays a premium (compensation) to the seller (writer of the option) for this right.

Key elements of options contracts include:

a) **Underlying Asset:** The type and quantity of the asset, whether stocks, commodities, currencies, or indices, must be specified in the contract.
b) **Strike Price:** The price at which the holder can exercise the option to buy or sell the underlying asset.

c) **Expiration Date:** The date on which the holder's right to exercise the option expires.
d) **Premium:** The amount paid by the option buyer to the writer, which is non-refundable regardless of whether the option is exercised.
e) **Negotiability:** Options are tradable financial instruments, deriving their value from the underlying asset.

- **Types of Options Contracts**

  a) By Nature of Contract:
  - **Call Option:** Grants the holder the right to buy a specified quantity of an asset at a predetermined price on or before the expiration date.
  - **Put Option:** Grants the holder the right to sell a specified quantity of an asset at a predetermined price on or before the expiration date.
  - **Complex Options:** These combine two or more basic options (call and put).

  b) By Ownership of the Underlying Asset:
  - **Covered Options:** The writer owns the underlying asset (e.g., securities or commodities) at the time of selling the option.
  - **Uncovered (Naked) Options:** The writer does not own the underlying asset and intends to acquire it later from the market to fulfil their obligation.

c) By Exercise Timing:
- **European Option**: This type of option can only be exercised on the expiration date, not before. The holder must wait until the expiration date to decide whether or not to exercise the option, which makes this a more limited but simpler option for investors.
  - **Advantages**: More straightforward pricing and strategy, as the exercise time is fixed.

- **Disadvantages**: Less flexibility in responding to favourable market conditions before the expiration date.

- **American Option**: This option can be exercised at any time before or on the expiration date. This added flexibility allows the holder to react to favourable price movements at any time during the life of the option.
  - **Advantages**: Greater flexibility in exercising the option, which can provide more opportunities for profit, especially in volatile markets.
  - **Disadvantages**: More complex pricing due to the flexibility to exercise at any point, and typically a higher premium than European options.

3.4.4.3 Swaps Contracts

A swaps contract involves the exchange of cash flows or other financial obligations between two parties. Unlike futures, where settlements occur daily, swaps are settled at the time of contract execution. These are often referred to as "paper profits and losses" until the swap is executed.

- **Types of Swaps Contracts**

A. **Interest Rate Swaps (Fixed-to-Floating):** One party pays a fixed interest rate while receiving a floating rate from the other party.
   - The fixed-rate payer hedges against rising interest rates.
   - The floating-rate payer hedges against falling interest rates.

B. **Caps Swaps (Unrestricted Floating Interest Rate):** The buyer receives the difference between the floating interest rate and the cap rate (strike price) if the floating rate exceeds the cap. If the floating rate is lower, no payments are made.

C. **Floors Swaps (Restricted Floating Interest Rate):** Floating-rate securities have a defined minimum and maximum rate. The buyer gains if the floating rate rises above the minimum. The writer pays the difference if the rate falls below the minimum.

D. **Mixed Swaps (Collars):** This involves a combination of caps and floors, where one party takes a long position on a cap and a short position on a floor. If the floating rate falls between the cap and floor, the contract functions as a fixed-rate swap.

3.4.4.4 Forward Contracts

Forward contracts are customised financial agreements between two parties to buy or sell a specific asset at a predetermined price on a specified future date. Unlike standardised futures contracts, forward contracts are private agreements, usually over-the-counter (OTC), and are not traded on exchanges.

These contracts are often tailored to meet the unique needs of the buyer and seller and are used to hedge risks or speculate on the price movements of the underlying asset.

- **Characteristics of Forward Contracts**
  - **Customisation:** Forward contracts are highly flexible and can be tailored to fit the specific requirements of the parties involved, including the asset type, quantity, delivery date, and location.
  - **No Standardisation:** Unlike futures contracts, forwards do not have standardised terms or require a central clearinghouse.
  - **OTC Trading:** These contracts are traded over-the-counter, making them less liquid compared to exchange-traded derivatives.
  - **Counterparty Risk:** Since there is no clearinghouse, there is a significant risk that one party may default on the agreement.
  - **No Mark-to-Market:** Forward contracts are not subject to daily settlement or margin requirements, and

gains or losses are realised only at the contract's maturity.

- **Underlying Assets:** Forwards can be based on various assets, including commodities, currencies, interest rates, or financial instruments.

- **Types of Forward Contracts**

A. By Underlying Asset:

- **Commodity Forward Contracts:** Agreements involving the future delivery of physical commodities like gold, oil, or wheat.
- **Currency Forward Contracts:** Contracts to exchange a specified amount of one currency for another at a future date. Commonly used for hedging foreign exchange risks.
- **Equity Forward Contracts:** Agreements to buy or sell equity securities or stock indices at a future date.
- **Interest Rate Forward Contracts:** Used to lock in interest rates for borrowing or lending in the future.

B. By Settlement Type:

- **Delivery-Based Forwards:** Require physical delivery of the underlying asset at the contract's expiration.
- **Cash-Settled Forwards:** Do not involve physical delivery but settle the contract by exchanging the cash difference between the agreed-upon forward price and the market price at maturity.

C. By Purpose:

- **Hedging Forward Contracts:** Designed to protect against price fluctuations of an underlying asset.
- **Speculative Forward Contracts:** Used by traders to profit from anticipated price movements.

- **Advantages and Disadvantages of Forward Contracts**
  - **Advantages**
    - Flexibility in terms of contract customisation.

    - Useful for hedging specific risks, such as currency or commodity price volatility.
    - No initial margin requirements or daily mark-to-market settlements.
    - Ideal for parties needing tailor-made financial agreements.
- **Disadvantages**
    - High counterparty risk due to lack of a clearinghouse.
    - Limited liquidity since contracts are not standardised or traded on exchanges.
    - Settlement risk, as the contract is fulfilled only at maturity.
    - Pricing challenges because forward rates depend on negotiated terms rather than market prices.

Chapter Four

Financial Market Efficiency

Chapter Four: Financial Market Efficiency

The concept of financial market efficiency has become a cornerstone of modern finance theory, influencing both academic research and practical investment strategies. At its core, market efficiency refers to the degree to which market prices reflect all available information. The idea suggests that in an efficient market, prices are set in such a way that it is impossible for an investor to consistently achieve higher returns than the overall market, given the information at hand. This notion has profound implications for how markets operate, how securities are valued, and how investors approach decision-making.

4.1 The Definition of Financial Market Efficiency The Efficient Market Hypothesis (EMH), developed by economist Eugene Fama in the 1960s, posits that financial markets are efficient in reflecting all available information in the prices of financial assets. According to Fama's theory, current prices of securities fully incorporate all known information, and therefore, it is impossible for investors to consistently achieve returns that exceed the market average using the available public or private information.

4.2 Types of Market Efficiency: Strong-Form and Economic Efficiency

Market efficiency, particularly as proposed by Eugene Fama in his Efficient Market Hypothesis (EMH), comes in different forms, each reflecting the level of information that is incorporated into asset prices. These forms are classified as weak-form, semi-strong form, and strong-form efficiency. Additionally, the concept of economic efficiency plays a critical role in determining the practical outcomes of market functioning, and how well markets allocate resources in the economy.

- **Strong-Form Efficiency (Full Information Efficiency)**

Strong-form efficiency represents the most stringent level of market efficiency. According to this form, all information—public and private—is fully reflected in asset prices. This implies that not only publicly available information (such as company earnings reports, economic data, etc.) but also private or insider information is already incorporated into the prices of securities.

In an ideally efficient market that exhibits strong-form efficiency, even insider trading would not yield abnormal profits because the information from insiders would already be embedded in the stock price. Therefore, in theory, no investor, regardless of their access to private or non-public information, could achieve higher returns than others consistently.

However, in practice, strong-form efficiency is often regarded as unrealistic because insider information is not always publicly available, and there are legal and ethical concerns surrounding its use. Moreover, regulatory frameworks in most countries prevent the illegal trading of insider information, further questioning the practical application of this form of market efficiency.

Key Features of Strong-Form Efficiency:

- All information, including private or insider information, is reflected in asset prices.
- No investor can earn abnormal returns using any information, whether public or private.
- In reality, strong-form efficiency is rarely observed, especially due to legal restrictions on insider trading.

- **Semi-Strong Form Efficiency (Public Information Efficiency)**

The semi-strong form of market efficiency suggests that asset prices reflect all publicly available information. This includes financial statements, earnings reports, news, government publications, and any other information that can be readily accessed by the public. According to this form, prices adjust quickly to new information as it becomes publicly available.

For instance, when a company releases its quarterly earnings report or when there is a significant change in government policy, the market reacts instantaneously to incorporate this new information into stock prices. If the market is semi-strong efficient, then investors cannot achieve abnormal returns by trading on publicly available information, as it is already reflected in stock prices.

This form of efficiency is more plausible than the strong-form version, as it acknowledges that insider information is not publicly accessible and thus not reflected in stock prices. However, it assumes that public information is swiftly and fully processed by the market, which may not always be the case due to human and institutional delays, errors in analysis, or the complex nature of information flow.

Key Features of Semi-Strong Form Efficiency:

- All publicly available information is incorporated into stock prices.
- Market prices adjust quickly and efficiently to new public information.
- Investors cannot consistently achieve abnormal returns from trading on publicly available information.

- **Weak-Form Efficiency (Past Prices Efficiency)**

Weak-form efficiency is the least restrictive form of market efficiency, stating that current asset prices reflect all past market data, such as historical prices and trading volumes. In this context, technical analysis, which relies on historical price patterns and trends to predict future prices, would not provide any advantage for investors looking to earn above-average returns.

According to weak-form efficiency, stock price movements are entirely random, meaning that past price movements cannot predict future price movements. Therefore, technical analysts who study historical price data would find that their strategies are no more effective than random guessing, as all relevant past information is already accounted for in the current price.

This form of efficiency is the most widely accepted, especially in academic circles, as it aligns with the concept of a "random walk," where price changes are independent of one another and follow a stochastic (random) process.

Key Features of Weak-Form Efficiency:

- Stock prices reflect all past trading data, such as historical prices and volumes.
- Technical analysis, which relies on past price data, cannot predict future price movements.
- The market follows a random walk, and price movements are unpredictable based on historical data alone.

- **Economic Efficiency (Resource Allocation Efficiency)**

While the above forms of efficiency focus on the incorporation of information into asset prices, economic efficiency concerns the optimal allocation of resources in the economy. In an economically efficient market, resources (including capital, labour, and goods) are allocated in such a way that maximises the total value of goods and services produced in the economy.

Economic efficiency in financial markets suggests that the funds raised through securities markets are used effectively to support productive investments, thereby contributing to economic growth and societal welfare. When financial markets are economically efficient, capital flows to the most productive and profitable ventures, supporting innovation, infrastructure development, and business expansion.

Economic efficiency is often linked to allocative efficiency, which refers to the ability of the market to distribute resources in a way that matches consumer preferences, and productive efficiency, which refers to the ability to produce goods and services at the lowest possible cost. A market that is economically efficient should ensure that firms can access funding easily, and that investors can allocate their capital optimally to achieve maximum returns.

Key Features of Economic Efficiency:

- Resources are allocated in a manner that maximises economic value.
- Financial markets support innovation and development by channelling funds to the most productive investments.
- A highly economically efficient market contributes to overall societal welfare and economic growth

According to Fama, in an efficient market, no investor can consistently outperform the market in the long run using any type of information, because all information is quickly and accurately reflected in asset prices.

4.3 Assumptions of Financial Market Efficiency

The concept of market efficiency, particularly as outlined by Eugene Fama in the Efficient Market Hypothesis (EMH), relies on a set of key assumptions that allow for the understanding and functioning of markets where asset prices reflect all available information. These assumptions are foundational to the theory and support the idea that it is impossible to consistently achieve above-average returns in an efficient market without taking on additional risk. Below are the main assumptions of financial market efficiency:

- **Rational Behaviour of Investors**: Investors are assumed to be rational and to make decisions that maximise their expected utility. This means that investors use all available information to make informed decisions and attempt to optimise their risk-return profile. In an efficient market, investors are presumed to react appropriately and promptly to new information. They act based on logical analysis rather than emotional impulses or irrational behaviour.
- **Access to Information:** It is assumed that all relevant information is readily and equally available to all market participants. This includes both public information, such as corporate earnings reports, and private or insider information. While the efficiency of the market can vary in practice (especially in terms of public versus private information), the assumption is that all information, once it is publicly disclosed, is quickly incorporated into asset prices.
- **No Transaction Costs:** The assumption of no transaction costs is fundamental to the EMH. This means that investors can buy and sell securities without incurring significant costs, such as brokerage fees, taxes, or bid-ask spreads. In reality, transaction costs exist, but they are assumed to be negligible in an efficient market. If transaction costs are too high, they could interfere with the process of price adjustment and lead to inefficiencies in the market.
- **Perfect Competition :** Markets are assumed to be perfectly competitive, where no single investor or institution has the power to influence the price of an asset. In such markets, there are numerous participants, and no

one player can manipulate prices. Prices are determined purely by supply and demand, ensuring that prices reflect all available information accurately.

- **Unlimited Arbitrage:** Arbitrage is the practice of exploiting price differences between markets or similar assets. In an efficient market, it is assumed that arbitrage opportunities are quickly exploited by market participants, eliminating any price discrepancies. For example, if an asset is mispriced in one market, arbitrageurs will buy the underpriced asset and sell it in a more expensive market, bringing prices into alignment. The assumption is that such opportunities are short-lived, and the process of arbitrage ensures that prices remain aligned with their true value.
- **Homogeneous Expectations:** The EMH assumes that all market participants have homogeneous expectations, meaning that they all interpret the available information in the same way. This assumption means that investors have a shared understanding of the future prospects of securities, and as a result, they react similarly to new information. In reality, different investors may interpret information differently, but the assumption of homogeneous expectations allows for the consistent pricing of assets in an efficient market.
- **Price Adjustment is Instantaneous**: In an efficient market, it is assumed that asset prices adjust instantaneously to new information. This means that as soon as new information becomes available, prices reflect the impact of that information without delay. In this idealised scenario, no investor can profit by trading on new information, as it would already be reflected in the market price by the time they act.
- **No Investor Has Inside Information**: The assumption of no insider information means that all investors have equal

access to the same information. In the case of semi-strong form efficiency, once public information is released, it is immediately incorporated into the market price, and no investor can gain an advantage by acting on it. In practice, however, insider trading does occur, which can lead to market inefficiencies and influence asset prices.

- **No Systematic Predictability**: The EMH assumes that there are no predictable patterns in asset prices that can be exploited by investors. This means that prices follow a random walk, and historical price data cannot be used to forecast future prices with consistent accuracy. The concept of randomness in price movements suggests that technical analysis, which relies on past price trends, would not be a useful tool for generating excess returns.
- **Investors Are Indifferent to Risk**: In an efficient market, it is assumed that all investors are equally willing to bear risk. This assumption underpins the idea that investors will make decisions based on expected returns, considering the level of risk associated with different investments. While in reality, investors may have varying risk preferences, this assumption is vital to ensure that market prices accurately reflect the expected risk-adjusted returns of assets.

4.4 Criticisms of the Efficient Market Hypothesis (EMH)

While the Efficient Market Hypothesis (EMH) has been a cornerstone of financial theory, it has also faced significant criticism over the years. Critics argue that the EMH fails to accurately reflect real-world market conditions and investor behaviour. Several alternative theories and models have emerged in response to the perceived shortcomings of the EMH.

- **Empirical Evidence Against the EMH** One of the main criticisms of EMH is the significant amount of empirical evidence that contradicts its predictions. Research has found that markets are often not as efficient as the hypothesis suggests. For example, studies have observed that stock prices do not always reflect all available information immediately. In fact, prices often exhibit patterns that can be predicted or exploited by certain market strategies.

- **Anomalies in the Market:** Several market anomalies, such as the January effect, value effect, and momentum effect, suggest that markets do not always follow the random walk implied by EMH. These anomalies are deviations from the efficient market model, indicating that asset prices may be influenced by factors beyond just publicly available information.
- **Behavioral Biases and Irrational Behaviour** EMH assumes that investors are rational and always make decisions based on available information. However, behavioral economics highlights that investors often act irrationally due to cognitive biases, emotional decision-making, and herd behaviour. Prospect theory, developed by Daniel Kahneman and Amos Tversky, challenges the assumption that investors always act in their best financial interest, as individuals tend to exhibit biases such as overconfidence, loss aversion, and framing effects.
- **Investor Herding Behaviour:** The tendency for investors to follow the crowd, particularly in moments of market excitement or fear, can lead to asset bubbles or crashes, which are not explained by EMH. Historical events such as the Dot-com Bubble and the Global Financial Crisis provide strong evidence of market behaviour that cannot be accounted for by the rationality assumption of EMH.
- **Limited Information Availability** EMH presumes that all investors have equal access to all information. In reality, however, access to information is often unequal. Certain investors, such as institutional investors or those

with insider information, have a distinct advantage over retail investors. This unequal access can result in a market that is not as efficient as the EMH suggests, as some participants may be able to act on information before it becomes available to the general public.

- **Market Overreaction and Underreaction** Another criticism of the EMH is the observation that markets sometimes overreact to news, leading to sharp price movements that eventually correct themselves. Conversely, markets may also underreact to news, causing prices to adjust slowly over time. These phenomena are inconsistent with the notion of an efficient market where prices are always quickly and accurately adjusted in response to new information.

  Examples of Overreaction and Underreaction:
  - **Overreaction**: The stock market often experiences excessive price movements following major announcements, such as earnings reports or political events. The tech bubble of the late 1990s is an example where market participants overvalued technology stocks.
  - **Underreaction**: There have been instances where markets fail to fully price in new information, such as when companies announce poor earnings, but the stock price declines slowly over time rather than immediately adjusting.
- **Excessive Volatility** EMH suggests that asset prices reflect all available information and thus should not be excessively volatile. However, the reality is that markets can experience periods of high volatility that cannot be explained by changes in fundamentals alone. This excessive volatility is a significant criticism of EMH, as it implies that asset prices may deviate from their true value

in ways that cannot be justified by the information available.

4.5 Alternative Theories and Models

In response to the criticisms of the EMH, several alternative theories have been developed to explain observed market behaviour more accurately. These theories either complement or oppose the efficient market model, offering a more nuanced understanding of financial markets.

- **The Fractal Market Hypothesis (FMH):** The Fractal Market Hypothesis (FMH) offers a robust alternative to the Efficient Market Hypothesis (EMH), proposing that financial markets are not fully efficient but instead exhibit fractal-like properties. The term fractal refers to self-replicating structures, meaning that similar patterns recur at different timeframes. According to FMH, markets operate with investors having different investment horizons, which results in various levels of volatility and liquidity.

  FMH argues that market instability occurs when the time horizons of long-term investors shorten due to information uncertainty, leading to a collective market decision that becomes less diverse and ultimately more prone to crashes. This is because when investors begin to interpret information in the same way (short-term and homogenous interpretations), the market becomes less diversified and prone to high volatility.

  The key components of FMH are:
  - Different Investment Horizons: Investors in the market have varied time horizons (short-term vs. long-term), and this leads to different interpretations of market data.
  - Market Stability and Liquidity: When these horizons are diverse, markets tend to be stable, as there is always a counterbalance between buyers and sellers.

- Crisis and Market Shocks: When long-term investors begin to question the validity of their information, they shorten their investment horizons, causing a uniformity in market sentiment that leads to instability.

FMH explains market cycles and suggests that market prices do not follow a normal distribution (as suggested by EMH) but instead exhibit fat tails—extreme events occurring more frequently than expected in traditional models.

- **Chaos Theory in Financial Markets:** Chaos Theory examines non-linear dynamic systems where small changes can have large, unpredictable effects. In the context of financial markets, Chaos Theory offers a framework to understand complex market behaviours, including the non-linearity of price movements and the unpredictable patterns observed in market dynamics. This theory contradicts the traditional assumption of randomness in financial markets and proposes that markets, though seemingly random, are actually governed by underlying deterministic laws.

The main principles of Chaos Theory in financial markets include:

- Non-linearity: Financial markets do not follow linear patterns, meaning that small shifts in inputs can lead to disproportionate market movements.
- Butterfly Effect: This principle suggests that tiny changes in initial conditions can lead to significant and unforeseen market outcomes. For example, a small news event can cause a massive market movement, reflecting the complexity of the market.
- Periodic Cycles: Chaos theory asserts that, despite appearing erratic, markets may exhibit cyclical patterns that repeat over time. These cycles, however, are not perfectly predictable.

Studies like those by LeBaron (1994) and Vaga (1994) have shown that financial markets exhibit non-linear behaviour, where small changes in variables (such as interest rates or commodity prices) can lead to large market changes, a phenomenon referred to as the "butterfly effect". This theory helps explain extreme market volatility and crashes that cannot be accounted for by traditional models like the EMH.

- **Complexity Theory in Financial Markets**

Complexity Theory challenges traditional economic models by recognising that financial markets are dynamic systems with interconnected elements, which cannot be fully understood using the assumptions of equilibrium-based economic models. Complexity theory posits that markets are adaptive systems—constantly evolving based on feedback loops and new information.

Key features of Complexity Theory in financial markets:

- Adaptation and Evolution: Market participants adjust their strategies over time based on the information they receive. Unlike in traditional models, the market does not reach an equilibrium but instead evolves as participants adapt to changing conditions.
- Interconnectedness: Different actors in the market (e.g., institutions, investors) are highly interconnected, and changes in one part of the system can trigger ripple effects throughout the market.
- Feedback Loops: Positive feedback loops can lead to bubbles and crashes, while negative feedback can stabilise the market. These feedback loops contribute to the market's non-linear behaviour.

The complexity model also incorporates adaptive agents, which are investors who update their behaviour in response to evolving market conditions. Unlike in traditional models that assume rational agents, complexity theory assumes that agents have limited knowledge and make decisions based on heuristics, which leads to market inefficiency.

- **Behavioural Finance:** Behavioural Finance challenges the rational investor assumption of traditional finance theories like the Efficient Market Hypothesis. It explores how psychological factors and cognitive biases influence investor behaviour, leading to market inefficiencies that are not explained by traditional models.

Key insights of Behavioural Finance:

- Cognitive Biases: Investors are often influenced by biases such as overconfidence, herding behaviour, and loss aversion, leading them to make decisions that deviate from rational financial theory.
- Market Anomalies: Behavioural finance helps explain anomalies in market behaviour, such as asset bubbles and excessive volatility, that EMH cannot account for.
- Emotions: Investor emotions, like fear and greed, significantly influence market decisions, leading to irrational price movements.
- Daniel Kahneman and Amos Tversky, pioneers in behavioural finance, demonstrated how investors' decisions are influenced by prospect theory—investors are more likely to make irrational choices when facing potential losses than when seeking gains, leading to market anomalies.

- **Adaptive Markets Hypothesis (AMH) :** The Adaptive Markets Hypothesis (AMH), introduced by Andrew Lo, provides a middle ground between the Efficient Market Hypothesis and Behavioural Finance. It proposes that financial markets are not perfectly efficient, but rather adaptive systems that evolve over time as investors adjust to changing conditions.

  Key ideas behind AMH:

- Evolutionary Processes: Just like in natural ecosystems, financial markets evolve through the interaction of market participants, who adapt to new challenges and opportunities.
- Market Efficiency is Dynamic: Rather than assuming that markets are always efficient, AMH posits that market efficiency fluctuates over time based on the behaviour of market participants.
- Learning Process: Investors learn from their experiences and adjust their strategies. As such, market efficiency is not a static condition but rather a result of the continual learning and adaptation of investors.

AMH provides a more flexible view of market behaviour, acknowledging that markets can be inefficient in some periods and efficient in others, depending on how investors adapt to changes in the environment.

Chapter Five
An Introduction to Investment Portfolios

Chapter Five: An Introduction to Investment Portfolios

Investment portfolios have become an essential aspect of modern financial management. The concept of a portfolio is deeply rooted in the goal of balancing risk and return, two fundamental components of any financial strategy. The creation and management of investment portfolios allow investors to optimize their returns by diversifying their investments across different financial instruments, thereby minimizing risk.

5.1 Origins of the Portfolio

The concept of investment portfolios emerged after 1952 when American analyst Harry Markowitz established the foundational principles of portfolio theory. He presented the first idea of a portfolio in his research titled "Portfolio Selection," illustrating how to construct an optimal portfolio that maximises expected returns while maintaining a certain level of risk. In 1962, William Sharpe advanced portfolio theory by introducing the Single-Index Model. This model addressed the question of what would happen if the portfolio model were adopted by all investors and how it would affect security prices in the financial market.

Building on this, Sharpe and Lintner introduced the Capital Asset Pricing Model (CAPM) in 1966, which became a benchmark for measuring portfolio efficiency. Later, in 1976, Ross refined this model into the Arbitrage Pricing Theory (APT), focusing on selecting securities by comparing returns and risks. Further contributions to portfolio theory were made in the late 20th century, spurred by economic developments, increased financial assets among corporations, banks, and savings funds, and the broader application of portfolio theory to the banking sector.

By the 1960s, the establishment of investment funds specialising in financial investments gained traction. While some of these funds failed due to poor management, others succeeded by employing effective portfolio management strategies. These successes led to the expansion of investment funds and the establishment of financial investment firms.

The goal of portfolio management is to compile diverse individual securities into a single investment portfolio and establish a relationship between the returns of these securities and their risks, measured by variations in returns.

5.2 Definition and Importance of Investment Portfolios

- **Definition of Investment Portfolios**: An investment portfolio is a collection of financial instruments and other investment tools. It represents a mix of assets owned by an investor, which may include both real and financial assets. The aim is to achieve the highest possible return with the least amount of risk, tailored to the investor's preferences—whether they are conservative, speculative, or rational. Portfolio management can either be conducted by the portfolio owner or by hired professionals.

From a theoretical perspective, a portfolio consists of a group of assets or investments. Portfolio theory addresses the problem of selecting optimal portfolios that maximise returns for a given level of risk or minimise risks for a specific level of return. The theory is primarily designed for financial assets like stocks and bonds.

Investment portfolios are carefully crafted sets of securities chosen to achieve specific objectives. These portfolios comprise various financial instruments like stocks and bonds, differing in terms of their value, the return they generate, and their maturity periods.

- **Importance of Investment Portfolios**

a) The increase in liquidity and financial surpluses among individual and corporate investors.
b) The expansion of mutual funds, financial institutions' portfolios, and the availability of diverse investment tools both locally and internationally.
c) Optimal utilisation of available financial resources through strategic investments in short-term and long-term financial instruments.

5.3 Types and Objectives of Investment Portfolios

- **Types of Investment Portfolios**

Investment portfolios can be categorised based on various factors:

a) **By Degree of Rigidity and Flexibility:**
   - **Fixed Portfolios:** These portfolios consist of specific securities chosen at the outset and listed as integral parts of the portfolio's foundational structure, often requiring general assembly approval for any changes.
   - **Semi-Fixed Portfolios:** These portfolios strike a balance between rigid and flexible portfolios, allowing limited adjustments to the securities within the portfolio while adhering to specific rules for reinvesting proceeds from sales.
   - **Flexible Portfolios:** Highly dynamic, these portfolios include a wide range of primary and secondary securities, offering substantial room for adjustments.

b) **By Objective:**
   - **Growth-Oriented Portfolios:** Designed to enhance the market value of the portfolio by focusing on high-growth securities, such as industrial company stocks.
   - **Income-Oriented Portfolios:** These portfolios aim to generate steady income for investors and typically include bonds and shares of stable companies that pay consistent dividends.

c) **Other Classifications:**
  - **Conservative Portfolios:** These ensure capital appreciation and stable returns while balancing short-term and long-term objectives.
  - **Security-Oriented Portfolios:** Prioritise preserving capital while ensuring a stable income, often favoured by insurance companies.
  - **Aggressive Portfolios:** Aim for significant returns, accepting higher risks and frequently adjusting to seize opportunities.
  - **Speculative Portfolios:** Focus on achieving rapid and high returns, involving substantial risk due to reliance on volatile securities.

- **Objectives of Investment Portfolios:**
  - **Growth Objective:** Focuses on maximising the portfolio's market value by prioritising high-growth stocks.
  - **Income Objective:** Ensures a steady income for investors to cover living expenses, often relying on stable bonds and shares of well-established companies.
  - **Balanced Objective:** Combines growth and income objectives by creating a mix of high-growth stocks and stable, income-generating securities such as treasury instruments.

5.4 Controls for Building a Financial Portfolio

A portfolio manager establishes several contracts and controls in advance, which are discussed with the portfolio owner to ensure they meet their needs, which are as follows:

- The investor must rely on their own capital to finance the portfolio without resorting to borrowing.
- There must be a portion of the portfolio consisting of low-risk company stocks once the investor has defined

the level of risk they can bear. It should also include a part with high-risk stocks that offer higher returns, based on the investor's ability to tolerate such risks.

- The investment time frame should be predetermined, and the type of investment should be defined in terms of its duration.
- The investor should periodically make changes to the portfolio components if their circumstances change, enabling them to bear greater risks or, conversely, reduce their exposure.
- Achieve an adequate level of diversification and assess portfolio performance against a relevant market index.

5.5 Constraints in Building a Securities Portfolio

To achieve the construction of an optimal financial portfolio, it is essential to consider the limitations and factors that influence the creation of such a portfolio.

- **First Constraint: The Importance of Portfolio Capital Growth:** This refers to the rate at which the capital of the portfolio increases during the investment period in the securities that make up the portfolio. If the goal is to increase the portfolio's capital in a short time, we seek an opportunity that provides a consistent growth rate. On the other hand, long-term investment means placing the portfolio's capital in securities that offer high growth rates over a longer period, although this is affected by many risks such as inflation rates. However, what matters here is not the slowdown of growth rates over a specific period, but rather the achievement of high growth rates over time.

Second Constraint" Return": Return refers to the total gains or losses resulting from an investment over a specified period. The financial portfolio focuses on return because every decision made reflects either a return or a loss. It is expressed as the added value the portfolio obtains, representing the change in the portfolio's wealth over a given time frame.

A key aspect of return is its calculation, particularly the Real Rate of Return, which considers the required return in the market, the Inflation Rate, and the Risk Premium. This calculation serves as the basis for determining the efficiency of portfolio management. Returns vary depending on when they are realised, and therefore, they must be addressed using a specific discount rate or the expected return rate. This expected rate incorporates the required return rate, inflation, and the risks associated with the cash flow during the investment period, which may cause deviations in return estimates from actual performance.

Several factors influence return, including the maturity period, the liquidity of securities, the risks associated with the return, and the tax rate borne by the portfolio. In addition, sunk costs, such as research, studies, and consultation fees incurred when seeking alternatives, also play a role in return estimation. Opportunity costs related to the use of available resources further contribute to the return calculation.

The return on securities can be measured according to their nature by calculating the Holding Period Yield (HPY). This measure reflects **the return realised** from the investment portfolio during the holding period of the securities. When analysing the components of return on securities, we observe that they come in two forms: current returns, such as dividends or interest, and capital gains, which result from the difference between the purchase price and the sale price of securities.

The **Holding Period Yield** can be calculated as follows:

$$R(HPY) = \frac{D_i + (P_t - P_{t-1})}{P_{t-1}} \qquad (1)$$

Where :

- D_i is the current expenses
- P_t is the sale price
- P_{t-1} is the purchase price

Example N°1: Suppose you made an investment in a particular stock. You purchased the stock at a price of £50, and subsequently sold it at a price of £60 after a certain period. During this period, you received dividends amounting to £2. Using the following data, calculate the Holding Period Yield (HPY)

Solution:

$$R(HPY) = \frac{D_i + (P_t + P_{t-1})}{P_{t-1}} = \frac{2 + (60 - 50)}{50} = 0.24$$

Thus, the Holding Period Yield (HPY) for this investment is 24%.

For a time series of returns, we use the arithmetic mean, which is known as the average return rate. This average is computed by averaging the returns over multiple periods.

$$\bar{R} = \frac{1}{T} \sum_{t=1}^{1+t-1} R \qquad (2)$$

Example N°2: Suppose you have invested in a portfolio over three years, and the returns for each year are as follows: In Year 1, the return was 8%. In Year 2, the return was 10%. In Year 3, the return was 6%.

Given this data, you can calculate the Average Return

Solution :

$\bar{R} = \frac{1}{T}\sum_{t=1}^{1+t-1} R$ *=1/3 (8+10+6)=0.08*

Thus, the average return for the portfolio over the three years is 8%. This represents the mean return generated by the portfolio over this period, helping assess its overall performance.

In the case of a portfolio composed of multiple securities n_i and priced at p_i, each security has a weight in the portfolio W_i:

$$Wi = \frac{\sum Purchasex}{Investment\ I} \qquad (3)$$

Where :

- W_i is the weight of the security in the portfolio.
- $\sum$*(Purchase x)* represents the sum of the purchases of the securities.
- *Investment I* is the total investment in the portfolio.

Example N°3 :Consider a portfolio composed of three securities with the following data:

Security	*Purchase Price (PiP_iPi)*	*Number of Units Purchased*
A	*£50*	*100*
B	*£30*	*200*
C	*£40*	*150*

The total investment in the portfolio is the sum of the purchases of all securities, which can be calculated as:

Total Investment$=(P_A\times$*Units of A*$)+(P_B\times$*Units of B*$)+(P_C\times$*Units of C*$)=(50\times100)+(30\times200)+(40\times150)$

$=5000+6000+6000=17000$

Now, to calculate the weight of each security in the portfolio, we use the formula:

$$Wi = \frac{\sum Purchasex}{Investment\ I}$$

For Security A (W_A): $W_A=(P_A\times$*Units of A*$)/$*Total Investment* $=(50\times100)/17000=0.2941$

The weight of Security A in the portfolio is 0.2941 or ***29.41%.***

For Security B (W_B): $W_B=(P_B\times$*Units of B*$)/$*Total Investment* $=(30\times200)/17000=0.3529$

The weight of Security B in the portfolio is 0.3529 or ***35.29%.***

For Security C (W_C): W_C=(PC×Units of C)/Total Investment =(40×150)/17000=0.3529

The weight of Security C in the portfolio is 0.3529 or ***35.29%.***

The portfolio's return can be defined as the weighted average return of the individual securities making up the portfolio:

$$R = \sum_{t=1}^{N} WiR \qquad (4)$$

Example N°4 : Suppose you have a portfolio consisting of three securities. Each security has a specific weight within the portfolio and a corresponding return. Consider the following data for the portfolio:

Security	*Weight (Wi)*	*Return (Ri)*
A	*0.4*	*8%*
B	*0.3*	*12%*
C	*0.3*	*6%*

Solution:

$R=(W_A \times R_A)+(W_B \times R_B)+(W_C \times R_C)$

$R=(0.4\times0.08)+(0.3\times0.12)+(0.3\times0.6)=0.086$

The portfolio return is **8.6%**

Expected Return and Variance : The expected return of a portfolio is typically linear. It is the weighted average of the different financial investments in the portfolio, which can be calculated based on two factors:

- The distribution of return probabilities across the portfolio.
- Future conditions (e.g., economic boom or recession).

The expected return is calculated as follows:

$$Ep = E(Rp) = \sum_{1-1}^{N} W_I E(R) \qquad (5)$$

Example N° 5: consider the following:

Event	*Probability*	*Return (%)*
1	*0.30*	*12*
2	*0.25*	*20*
3	*0.45*	*15*

The expected return is:
Ep=12(0.30)+20(0.25)+15(0.45)=3.6+5+6.75=15.35

Figure 1: Distribution of Return Based on the Example

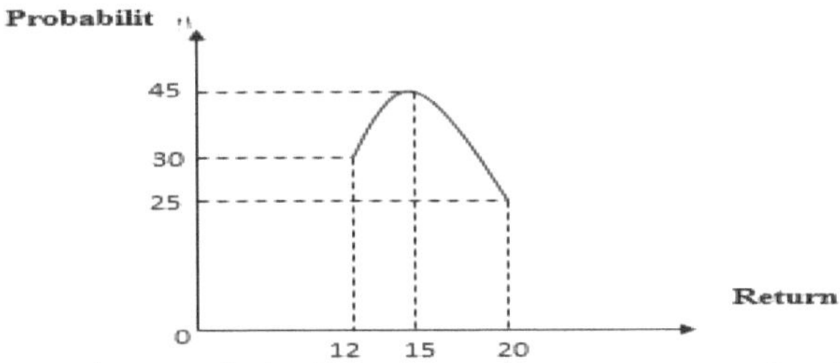

Variance: is a statistical measure that represents the degree of spread in the returns of a security or portfolio around its expected return. It indicates how much the returns deviate from the average (mean) return over a specific period. A higher variance indicates that the returns are more spread out, reflecting a higher level of risk, whereas a lower variance suggests that the returns are more concentrated around the mean, indicating lower risk.

The formula for calculating the variance of returns R is:

$$\text{Var}(R_P) = \delta_p^2(R_P) = \frac{1}{N-1}\sum_{t=1}^{n}[(R_t - \bar{R})^2] \quad (6)$$

Where:

- *Var(R) is the variance of the returns.*
- *R_t is the return at time t.*
- *$\bar{R}$The mean return.*
- *N is the number of time periods.*

Example N° 6: Suppose you have the following returns for a stock over three years:

Year	Return (R_t)
1	8%
2	10%
3	6%

Solution:

$$\bar{R} = \frac{8 + 10 + 6}{3} = 8\%$$

$$\text{Var}(R_P) = \frac{1}{3 - 1}\left[(8 - 8)^2 + (10 - 8)^2 + (6 - 8)^2\right] = 4$$

The variance of 4 indicates the degree of variability in the stock's returns. A higher variance would indicate that the returns are more spread out, and thus the stock is more volatile or risky. Conversely, a lower variance would indicate that the returns are more stable.

When probabilities are involved, variance can be calculated using the weighted probabilities of each return. This is typically the case when we are dealing with non-equal probabilities for different outcomes. The formula for calculating the variance of returns with probabilities P_i is:

$$\text{Var}(R_P) = \delta_p^2(R_P) = \sum_{t=i}^{n} P_i[(R_i - \bar{R})^2] \qquad (7)$$

Where:

- *Var(R)* is the variance of the returns.
- P_i is the probability of each return.
- R_i is the return for each outcome.
- $\bar{R}$ is the mean return.
- N is the number of possible outcomes.

Example N°7: Suppose you have the following returns for a stock over three possible outcomes, with their respective probabilities:

Event	Probability (P_i)	Return (R_i)
1	0.30	12%
2	0.25	20%
3	0.45	15%

Solution:

$\bar{R} = (0.3 \times 0.12) + (0.25 \times 0.2) + (0.45 \times 0.15) = 0.1535$

$\text{Var}(R_P) = 0.3(0.12\text{-}0.1535)^2 + 0.25(0.20\text{-}0.1535)^2 + 0.45(0.15\text{-}0.1535)^2 = 8.8275$

Covariance Between Two Returns: Covariance measures the degree to which two random variables (in this case, returns on two securities) move together. It is a critical metric in portfolio theory as it helps assess the relationship between the returns of different assets in the portfolio. If the covariance is positive, the two assets tend to move in the same direction, while a negative covariance indicates that the assets move in opposite directions.

The formula for covariance between two returns R_A and R_B is given by:

$$cov(R_A + R_B) = \frac{1}{N-1}\sum_{t=1}^{n}\{(R_A - \bar{R}_A).(R_B - \bar{R}_B)\} \quad (8)$$

Where:

- $cov(R_A, R_B)$ is the covariance between the returns of securities A and *B*
- R_A and R_B are the mean returns of securities A and B, respectively.
- N is the number of periods (for example, years or quarters) over which the returns are measured.

Interpretation of Covariance:

- Positive Covariance: If the covariance between two assets is positive, this means that the returns on these assets tend to move in the same direction. When the return on one asset rises, the return on the other asset tends to rise as well.

- Negative Covariance: If the covariance is negative, this suggests an inverse relationship between the returns of the two assets. When the return on one asset increases, the return on the other tends to decrease.
- Zero Covariance: A covariance of zero indicates no linear relationship between the returns of the two assets. The assets are considered to be independent of each other in terms of their returns.

Why is Covariance Important in Portfolio Theory?

Covariance is used to understand how different assets in a portfolio interact with each other. A well-diversified portfolio benefits from assets with negative or low positive covariance because the overall risk of the portfolio can be reduced when the assets do not move in perfect harmony. Conversely, if the assets have high positive covariance, the portfolio's risk may be higher, as the assets are more likely to experience similar fluctuations in value.

Example N° 8: Let's assume we have the following returns for two securities

Year	R_A *(%)*	R_B *(%)*
1	*8*	*6*
2	*10*	*12*
3	*6*	*4*

Solution:

The mean return for each security is calculated as:

$$\overline{R_A} = \frac{8 + 10 + 6}{3} = 8\%$$

$$\overline{R_B} = \frac{6 + 12 + 4}{3} = 7.33\%$$

Now, we apply the covariance formula to find the covariance between

$$cov(R_A + R_B) = \frac{1}{N-1}\sum\nolimits_{t=1}^{n} \{(R_A - \bar{R}_A).(R_B - \bar{R}_B)\}$$
$$= \frac{1}{3-1}\{(8-8)(6-7.33)$$
$$+ (10-8)(12-7.33) + (6-8)(4-7.33)\}$$
$$= 8$$

*The result of the covariance calculation between R_A and R_B is **8**. This indicates the degree to which the returns on securities A and B move together.*

- **The Third Factor Constraint" Risk " :**Risk refers to the possibility of losing some or all of an investment. Every investor has a unique and varied level of tolerance towards risk. Webster defines risk as "the chance of suffering harm, damage, or loss.

Generally, risks are associated with the uncertainty of future events, and they can be classified into several categories. In this research, we will divide risks into two main types:

A. Systematic Risks: These represent the portion of risk related to the overall movement of the market, and they are considered as the total risk impacting the financial markets. Changes in the economic, political, and social environment affect the financial markets.

Sources of Systematic Risks:

- **Market Risk**: Refers to the overall movement of security prices in the market. These prices tend to move together in response to external events (events not primarily linked to the companies involved). When a movement occurs in the market for a stock, whether up or down, an investor cannot do much to avoid these short-term fluctuations in stock prices caused by those events.
- **Interest Rate Risk**: Refers to the variability in returns resulting from changes in interest rates. Generally, market interest rates tend to rise or fall together in the long term.

Changes in interest rates affect bonds and fixed-income securities, causing their prices to move in the opposite direction to interest rates.

- **Purchasing Power Risk**: Refers to the possibility of a decline in the purchasing power of savings or invested wealth due to inflation. Purchasing power risk affects fixed-income securities, particularly when inflation rates exceed fixed interest rates. Common stocks, however, tend to change to a lesser extent than fixed-income securities and can provide partial protection against inflation.
- **Leverage Risk**: Leverage is measured by the ratio of debt to equity or the ratio of debt to total assets. Assuming all else remains constant, the variability in shareholder returns increases with the use of leverage. As a result, the company's fixed interest expenses rise, and the earnings volatility increases due to fluctuations in the company's sales. This reflects fluctuations in stock prices. The leverage can be calculated as follows:

$$\text{Leverage} = \frac{\text{EBIT}}{\text{Net Income}} = \frac{\text{Operating Income}}{\text{Net Income After Taxes}} \qquad (9)$$

Where:

- *EBIT*: Earnings Before Interest and Taxes (also known as operating profit).
- *Net Income*: The profit after taxes, also referred to as the final profit.

To measure the effect of financial leverage on profit changes, we use the following formula:

$$Percentage\ Change\ in\ Net\ Income = Leverage \times Percentage\ Change\ in\ EBIT \qquad (10)$$

If there is a change in operating profit (EBIT), financial leverage magnifies this change in net income (after taxes).

- **Operating Leverage Risk**: Operating leverage risk is measured by the ratio of the company's fixed costs to its variable costs. It relates to the structure of a company's costs, particularly the proportion of fixed costs to total costs. The higher the value of operating leverage, the greater the variation in earnings per share, meaning that a small decline in sales will lead to a significant decrease in operating profit.

  The change in operating profit (EBIT) can be expressed as a function of the operating leverage and the change in sales:

$$Change\ in\ Operating\ Profit = Operating\ Leverage \times Change\ in\ Sales \tag{11}$$

Where:

- *Operating Leverage* measures the sensitivity of operating profit (EBIT) to changes in sales.
- *Change in Sales* refers to the percentage change in the sales volume.

A higher operating leverage indicates that even a small change in sales can result in a significant change in operating profit, due to the presence of high fixed costs in the company's cost structure.

B. Unsystematic Risks: Unsystematic risk refers to the portion of total risk that is unique to a particular security or firm. It is the risk that can be reduced or eliminated through diversification. The sources of unsystematic risk include:

- **Economic Risks**: These reflect the risks associated with the overall economic environment, such as business cycle fluctuations.
- **Business Risks**: These involve the uncertainty surrounding a company's ability to generate satisfactory

returns from its investments. It also relates to various cost and revenue factors considered when determining that return.

- **Financial Risks**: Primarily related to a company's capital structure and its ability to meet its obligations and fixed expenses. It is concerned with short-term liquidity and the capacity to repay long-term obligations.
- **Management Risks**: Management can cause unique and irregular fluctuations in returns. Significant management errors, including the company's strategy and future direction, could even lead to bankruptcy. Common management errors include being unprepared for crises, lacking foresight, and failing to handle energy crises and labour strikes effectively.
- **Industry Risks**: Companies within the same industry or sector are exposed to risks that could alter returns due to factors that do not affect most companies outside that industry. These are called industry-specific risks. Sources of industry risk can include disruptions in raw material supply, anti-pollution laws, the impact of foreign competition, the emergence of new products or technologies, and changes in consumer behaviour in developed economies.
- **Risk Measurement of Financial Assets and Portfolios**

The risk associated with a financial asset can be measured in several ways, including using variance, standard deviation, coefficient of variation, and beta.

-The variance for a single asset has been addressed in Equation (7) above.

-The risk of a portfolio composed of two assets is measured by the variance, which is given by the following formula:

$$\text{Variance of Portfolio} = W_1^2 Var(R_1) + W_2^2 Var(R_2) + 2\, W_1 . W_2 . Cov(R_1, R_2) \qquad (12)$$

Where :

- W_1, W_2 are the weights of the two assets in the portfolio.
- $Var(R_1), Var(R_2)$ are the variances of the returns of the two assets.
- $Cov(R_1,R_2)$ is the covariance between the returns of the two assets.

- The risk of a portfolio composed of N financial assets is measured by the variance, which is calculated by the following equation:

$$\text{Variance of Portfolio} = \sum_{i=1}^{N} W_1^2 \; Var(R_i) + \sum_{i \neq j} W_i . W_j . Cov(R_i, R_j) \qquad (13)$$

$$\delta_{Rp}^2 = (x_1, x_2, x_3, \ldots\ldots\ldots, x_n) \begin{bmatrix} \delta_{11} & \delta_{12} & . & . & . & \delta_{1n} \\ \delta_{21} & \delta_{22} & . & . & . & \delta_{2n} \\ . & . & . & . & . & . \\ . & . & . & . & . & . \\ \delta_{n1} & \delta_{n2} & . & . & . & \delta_{nn} \end{bmatrix} \begin{bmatrix} x_1 \\ x_2 \\ . \\ . \\ x_n \end{bmatrix}$$

Where :

- Wi is the weight of asset i in the portfolio.
- $Var(Ri)$ is the variance of the return of asset i.
- $Cov(Ri,Rj)$ is the covariance between the returns of assets i and j.

Standard Deviation is defined as the square root of the variance, denoted as δ, where:

$$\delta_p = \sqrt{\sum_{t=i}^{n} P_i[(R_i - \overline{R})^2]} \qquad (14)$$

The standard deviation of a portfolio consisting of N financial assets can be found by taking the square root of the variance.

Risk associated with a particular investment is understood by observing changes in the rate of return. The greater the fluctuations in these rates, or in other words, the wider the probability distribution curve of returns (measured by variance or standard deviation), the higher the risk. Conversely, a lower variance or standard deviation means lower risk exposure.

Coefficient of Variation: can be used instead of the standard deviation as a measure of risk, especially when comparing assets with different return magnitudes. This is particularly useful when the standard deviation of two assets might be equal, but the percentage deviation of one asset's returns may be larger than the other.

The coefficient of variation is calculated by dividing the standard deviation by the mean return, as shown below:

$$CV = \frac{\delta}{\bar{R}} \tag{15}$$

The risk of a portfolio can also be measured using the coefficient of variation by dividing the portfolio's standard deviation by the expected return:

$$CV_{portfolio} = \frac{\delta_{Portfolio}}{\bar{R}_{portfolio}} \tag{16}$$

Where:

- $\bar{R}_{portfolio}$ is the expected return of the portfolio.

The coefficient of variation provides a measure of the relative risk per unit of return. A higher coefficient of variation indicates higher risk relative to return.

Beta : is a statistical measure of systematic risk and gauges the sensitivity of a security's return to the return of the market portfolio. It measures the degree to which a particular asset's return moves in line with the overall market's return.

To calculate Beta, the covariance between the return of the security and the return of the market portfolio is needed. This is given by the following equation:

$$B_X = \frac{Cov(R_x.R_m)}{\delta^2_{Rm}} = \frac{r(R_x.R_m)(\delta_{Rx})(\delta_{Rm})}{\delta^2_{Rm}} = \frac{r(R_x.R_m)(\delta_{Rx})}{\delta_{Rm}} \tag{17}$$

Where:

- $Cov(R_x, R_m)$ is the covariance between the return of the asset and the market return.
- δ^2_{RM} the variance of the market returns.

Beta reflects how much the asset's return is likely to change relative to the market's return. If $\beta=1$, the asset's return moves in line with the market. If $\beta>1$, the asset is more volatile than the market, and if $\beta<1$, the asset is less volatile than the market

The risk of a portfolio can also be measured by the beta of the portfolio, which is the weighted average of the individual betas of the assets in the portfolio

Where:

$$\beta_{\text{portfolio}} = \sum_{i=1}^{N} W_i \, \beta_i \tag{18}$$

- β_i is the beta of asset i.
- W_i is the weight of asset i in the portfolio.

It is important to note that the market beta is equal to one. Therefore, any portfolio with a beta of one will have risks equal to the market's risks. A portfolio with a beta less than one will have lower risks than the market, while a portfolio with a beta greater than one will have higher risks than the market.

Example N° 9: uppose you have two stocks, Stock A and Stock B, and you want to measure their risks using Standard Deviation, Coefficient of Variation, and Beta. Below are the returns for both stocks over the past five years:

Year	*Return A(%)*	*Return B(%)*
1	*10*	*6*
2	*12*	*8*
3	*8*	*10*
4	*15*	*5*
5	*9*	*7*

Solution:

$$\overline{RA} = \frac{10 + 12 + 8 + 15 + 9}{5} = 10.8\%$$

$$\overline{RB} = \frac{6 + 8 + 10 + 5 + 7}{5} = 7.2\%$$

Stock A has a higher standard deviation (2.48%) compared to Stock B (1.72%), indicating that Stock A is more volatile and carries greater risk.

Pi is the probability (in this case, each year has equal probability, so Pi=1/5

$\delta_A{}^2 = \frac{1}{5}((10 - 10.8)^2 + (12-10.8)^2 + (8-10.8)^2 + (15-10.8)^2 + (9-10.8)^2) = 6.16$, $\delta_A = \sqrt{6.16} = 2.48\%$, $CV_A = \frac{2.48}{10.8} = 0.23$

$\delta_B{}^2 = \frac{1}{5}((6 - 7.2)^2 + (8-7.2)^2 + (10-7.2)^2 + (5-7.2)^2 + (7-7.2)^2) = 2.9$, $\delta_B = \sqrt{2.96} = 1.72\%$ $CV_B = \frac{1.72}{7.2} = 0.24$

The coefficient of variation for Stock A (0.23) is slightly lower than Stock B (0.24), indicating that Stock A has a slightly more efficient risk-to-return ratio than Stock B.

-Assume the covariance between the returns of the stocks and the market is as follows:

- *Covariance of Stock A with Market = 0.04*

- *Covariance of Stock B with Market = 0.03*
- *The variance of the market return = 0.02*

$\beta_A = 0.04/0.02 = 2.0$

$\beta_B = 0.03/0.02 = 1.5$

Beta for Stock A is 2.0, which means it is twice as volatile as the market, whereas Stock B has a beta of 1.5, meaning it is 1.5 times as volatile as the market.

Comparison of the Results:

Measure	*Stock A*	*Stock B*
Standard Deviation	*2.48%*	*1.72%*
Coefficient of Variation (CV)	*0.23*	*0.24*
Beta	*2.0*	*1.5*

By calculating Standard Deviation, Coefficient of Variation, and Beta, we can assess the relative risk and volatility of both stocks. In this case, Stock A is more volatile and carries a higher risk, but Stock B has a slightly higher risk-to-return ratio when compared to its mean return.

Chapter Six
Portfolio Management and Administration Strategies

Chapter Six: Portfolio Management and Administration Strategies

This chapter delves into a crucial aspect of financial portfolio management, focusing on the effective administration of portfolios through the strategies, policies, and decision-making processes involved. It expands beyond the traditional concept of a portfolio to explore the methods employed in determining and implementing appropriate plans aimed at achieving optimal investment performance in a dynamic financial environment.

6.1 Objectives of Portfolio Management

Portfolio management aims to achieve the highest return with the lowest level of risk while ensuring liquidity, meaning managing funds with minimal possible losses. The key objectives of portfolio management are:

- **Capital Preservation:** One of the primary objectives of portfolio management is to preserve the original capital. While investing in financial securities inherently involves accepting risk, it is crucial to avoid jeopardising the original capital. Portfolio managers focus on maintaining the real value of the portfolio's capital, which is vital to protect against the erosion of wealth due to market fluctuations. Ensuring capital preservation allows investors to maintain their initial investment and build upon it with minimal risk exposure.
- **Achieving Optimal Return with Minimal Risk:** A key goal of portfolio management is to achieve the best possible return for a given level of risk. This requires balancing the risk-return trade-off, where managers aim to optimise the portfolio's performance. Risk is minimised while striving for the highest possible return, ensuring the investor's financial goals are met without exposing them

to excessive risk. This involves selecting appropriate financial instruments that align with the investor's risk tolerance and return expectations.

- **Ensuring Liquidity:** is an essential consideration in portfolio management. It refers to the portfolio's ability to convert its assets into cash without incurring significant losses. Managers must ensure that the portfolio includes financial instruments that can be easily liquidated in case of financial distress or unforeseen circumstances. Maintaining a sufficient level of liquidity allows the portfolio to meet immediate cash needs while safeguarding the overall value of the investment.
- **Continuous Income Generation:** Portfolio management aims to secure a continuous income stream for the investor. This involves selecting investments that provide regular cash inflows, such as dividends, interest, or rent, depending on the nature of the securities. A portfolio that generates a steady income ensures that the investor's ongoing financial needs are met, whether for living expenses or for reinvestment purposes. Moreover, ensuring consistent income helps to cover operational costs, thus contributing to the portfolio's long-term sustainability.
- **Diversification:** is a core principle of portfolio management. It involves spreading investments across different asset classes, such as stocks, bonds, or real estate, to reduce risk. By diversifying, the portfolio manager can mitigate the impact of poor performance from any single asset. This reduces the overall risk of the portfolio because the assets in the portfolio do not tend to move in the same direction under all market conditions. Proper diversification helps balance risk and return, achieving more stable performance over time.

- **Marketability of Securities:** An important objective of portfolio management is ensuring the marketability of the securities within the portfolio. This refers to the ability of the portfolio to be traded in the financial markets, or the ease with which assets can be converted into cash when needed. Having marketable securities in the portfolio means the investor can access liquidity quickly and efficiently, which is especially important in times of market volatility or personal financial need. Ensuring the portfolio is made up of liquid and tradable instruments allows the investor to manage both planned and unexpected financial requirements.

6.2 Methods of Portfolio Management

There are several types of portfolio management methods, which are as follows:

- **Direct Management:** Direct management refers to portfolios that are formed based on the investor's requests, giving them the right to manage the portfolio, issue buy and sell orders, and trade financial instruments. The investor must have expertise in financial matters. Optimal portfolio management requires the investor to monitor national and international financial markets daily and have complete knowledge of various financial instruments. Moreover, portfolio management does not mean randomly selecting a group of financial instruments, but rather follows an investment strategy aimed at forming a mix of alternatives and the most effective investment opportunities.
- **Advisory Management:** If the investor lacks experience and specialization in investment principles and rules, they may turn to specialists for financial advice regarding investments in the stock market (Le Conseil professionnel). However, the final investment decision

remains with the investor. The investor may also enter into a contract to deposit financial instruments and have them returned upon request, with the management of these instruments being handled by the investor themselves.

- **Portfolio Account Management:** In this type of contract, the investor appoints an intermediary to manage the portfolio account. There are two types of contracts:
  - Agency Contract: If the financial instruments are nominal.
  - Contract of Assignment: If the financial instruments are bearer securities. In both cases, the financial intermediary is responsible only for executing the management tasks and not for making decisions. Their obligation is limited to providing advice.
- **Full Management (Gestion déléguée):** In full management, the investor delegates their portfolio management to a specialized company. The company is entrusted with developing and executing an investment plan in the stock market. This contract is known as a management under agency and is an independent form of portfolio management.
- **Collective Management (La gestion collective):** This type of management is used for small investors, who can hold instruments issued by investment funds. These funds use the savings to form a portfolio of financial instruments and manage it according to technical and legal rules. Collective management means that the portfolio is not owned by a single investor, but by a large group of investors.

6.3 Portfolio Management Strategies

Studies have shown that managing portfolios does not require focusing solely on selecting the components of the portfolio from securities to achieve diversified investment returns; this can be achieved through various strategies, the most important of which are:

6.3.1 Active Strategies (Dynamic Approach)

These strategies focus on continuous monitoring and adjusting the portfolio to outperform the market. They require a belief that the market is not fully efficient, and involve frequent changes in the portfolio based on predictions and market movements.

- **Shares Management (Active Strategy) :** The portfolio manager actively monitors security prices and attempts to beat the market. This requires market timing, which involves predicting the best moments to buy or sell securities. Methods of Active Strategy Management:
  - Time the Market Method: The investor moves funds between stocks and bonds, based on market predictions.
  - Sector Rotation Method: Funds are moved between sectors, such as industrial, service, or financial sectors, to capitalize on sector performance.
  - Stock Picking Method: The investor targets undervalued stocks, buying low and selling high.
- **Bond Management (Active Strategy):** Active strategies for bonds involve moving funds and making adjustments based on market forecasts and expected price movements. Methods of Active Bond Management:
  - Market Timing Strategy: Funds are shifted between short-term and long-term bonds based on predictions about interest rates or other market conditions.
  - Sector Rotation Strategy: Allocate funds between different types of bonds (government, corporate, municipal) based on sector performance expectations.

- Bond Picking Strategy: Identify undervalued bonds and select them for investment based on their potential for appreciation.

Example N°10: You are managing a portfolio that includes both stocks and bonds. Based on recent market analysis, you expect some sectors to perform well, while others may experience a downturn. Additionally, you have predictions about interest rate changes and bond price movements. Your goal is to use active strategies to outperform the market. Below are the details and methods to apply.

Scenario:

- *Stock Portfolio:*
  - *Company A: Price has increased by 10% over the past month.*
  - *Company B: Price has decreased by 5% over the past month.*
  - *Company C: Price has remained stable.*
- *Bond Portfolio:*
  - *Short-Term Bonds (STB): Interest rates are expected to rise.*
  - *Long-Term Bonds (LTB): Interest rates are expected to fall.*

Methods for Active Strategy:

- *Time the Market Method: You need to decide whether to move funds between stocks and bonds based on the predictions for each asset class.*
  - *Stocks: You believe the price of Company A will continue to rise, while Company B may face more losses.*
  - *Bonds: You expect that Short-Term Bonds will underperform due to rising interest rates, while Long-Term Bonds will benefit from falling interest rates.*
- *Sector Rotation Method: You can move funds between sectors to capitalize on the strongest performers.*

- *You believe that the technology sector will outperform the energy sector in the next quarter.*
- *You want to move funds from energy-related stocks to technology-related stocks.*

- *Stock Picking Method: You need to pick undervalued stocks based on their potential for price appreciation.*
  - *Company A is predicted to continue its growth, but you believe Company C is undervalued and will see future growth.*
- *Bond Market Timing: You need to shift funds between Short-Term Bonds (STB) and Long-Term Bonds (LTB).*
  - *With interest rates rising, it may be prudent to move funds out of Short-Term Bonds and into Long-Term Bonds to lock in lower rates for a longer period.*

Task:

1. *Portfolio Rebalancing: Based on the above methods, how would you adjust the portfolio allocation between stocks and bonds?*
   - *Allocate funds between stocks (Company A, B, C) and bonds (STB, LTB).*
2. *Sector Rotation Strategy: How would you allocate funds between the technology sector and the energy sector?*
   - *Decide the percentage of funds to move from the energy sector to the technology sector.*
3. *Stock Picking Strategy: Which stocks would you target for buying low and selling high?*
   - *Select Company A and/or Company C based on your analysis of future price appreciation.*
4. *Bond Management Strategy: How would you allocate funds between Short-Term Bonds (STB) and Long-Term Bonds (LTB) based on the interest rate predictions?*

Solution:

1. Portfolio Rebalancing: Given that you expect Company A to continue rising, and Company B to face more losses, you should:

- *Sell a portion of Company B and reinvest in Company A.*
- *Shift funds from Short-Term Bonds (STB) to Long-Term Bonds (LTB) based on the interest rate prediction (falling rates for LTB).*

Asset Class	*Current Allocation*	*New Allocation*	*Action*
Company A	*30%*	*40%*	*Increase allocation*
Company B	*30%*	*10%*	*Sell part of Company B*
Company C	*40%*	*50%*	*Maintain allocation*
STB	*50%*	*30%*	*Sell part of STB*
LTB	*50%*	*70%*	*Increase allocation*

2. Sector Rotation Strategy: You believe the technology sector will outperform the energy sector. Hence, you should:

- *Sell some of the energy sector stocks.*
- *Buy technology sector stocks with the funds raised.*

Sector	*Current Allocation*	*New Allocation*	*Action*
Technology	*20%*	*40%*	*Buy more technology stocks*
Energy	*40%*	*20%*	*Sell energy sector stocks*
Other Sectors	*40%*	*40%*	*Maintain allocation*

3. Stock Picking Strategy:

You believe Company C is undervalued and will appreciate in the future, so you should:

- *Buy more of Company C, as it has high potential for future price growth.*

Stock	*Current Allocation*	*New Allocation*	*Action*
Company A	*40%*	*40%*	*Maintain allocation*
Company B	*10%*	*10%*	*Maintain allocation*
Company C	*50%*	*60%*	*Increase allocation*

4. Bond Management Strategy: Based on rising interest rates, you would:

- *Sell Short-Term Bonds (STB), as their value is likely to decrease with higher rates.*
- *Buy more Long-Term Bonds (LTB) to benefit from the falling rates.*

Bond Type	*Current Allocation*	*New Allocation*	*Action*
STB	*50%*	*30%*	*Sell part of STB*
LTB	*50%*	*70%*	*Increase LTB allocation*

Example N° 11: An investment firm buys government bonds worth £1,000 with a 6% annual interest rate (fixed rate). The investment is made for a period of 8 years. The firm expects the interest rates to change in the following manner: 8%, 6%, and 4% for the next three years. The firm plans to reassess the portfolio and adapt it based on these changes. The goal is to determine the effect of these interest rate changes on the bond value.

Interest Rate (%)	*8%*	*6%*	*4%*
Starting Value (£)	*1,000*	*1,000*	*1,000*

Task:

1-Calculate the bond value at each interest rate change over the years.

2- Find the difference between the final value and starting value for each period.
Solution:
1- Calculate the Initial Value of the Bond:
The starting value of the bond is £1,000, with an interest *rate of 6%. The bond pays a 6% annual interest, which means the coupon (C) is:* $C=1,000\times6\%=£60$
2-*Determine the Value of Bonds in the Future:*
The firm wants to know how the change in interest rates will affect the bond's value over time. The formula used for bond valuation with interest changes is: $V=C/(1+r)^n$

Interest Rate (%)	*8%*	*6%*	*4%*
Starting Value (£)	*1,000*	*1,000*	*1,000*
Final Value (£)	$60/(1+0.08)$ $=£944.44$	$60/(1+0.06)^2$ $=£891.01$	$60/(1+0.04)^3$ $=£837.68$
Change (£)	*-£55.56*	*-£53.43*	*-£53.33*

As the interest rates decrease, the market value of the bond also decreases.
The active bond strategy involves reassessing the portfolio and making adjustments based on market changes.

6.3.2 Static Strategy (Traditional Approach)

Passive (Static) Strategies are based on the assumption that markets are efficient, meaning that bond and stock prices reflect all available information, making it difficult to consistently outperform the market. Therefore, these strategies aim for long-term stability by holding bonds and stocks with predetermined characteristics, with minimal adjustments made to the portfolio. Investors follow a buy-and-hold policy for relatively long periods, focusing on adequate diversification and determining an acceptable level of risk. Continuous alteration of portfolio components is not deemed necessary, as market efficiency suggests that extraordinary profits occur by chance rather than through active intervention. Consequently, passive strategies seek to achieve balanced and stable returns by maintaining a portfolio that aligns with the investor's risk tolerance and long-term objectives.

- **Stock Management Methods**:
  - Full Replication Method: In this method, the investor constructs a portfolio that exactly mirrors the price index, purchasing the same stocks in the same proportions as the index. It is important to note that this method requires the investor to reinvest any dividends from their investments into the same components of the portfolio, maintaining the same investment ratios. Furthermore, the investor must continuously monitor changes in the index components and reflect these changes in the portfolio. However, this method has two significant drawbacks:
    - The investor must invest in a large number of securities.
    - Reinvesting dividends accurately may be challenging, and additional commissions are incurred during the reinvestment process.
  - Sampling Method: Given the limitations of full replication, some investors may choose to use the sampling method to replicate the index based on statistical principles. In this approach, the investor does not expect the portfolio's returns to exactly match those of the index, but aims to achieve a reasonable representation of its performance.
  - Stock Picking Method: In this method, the investor selects a group of strategic investments to buy and hold for the long term, based on the returns they offer and their potential for market value appreciation. The

investor aims for a reasonable return that aligns with the level of risk they are willing to bear. This method may also involve investing in a mutual fund with specific characteristics that align with the investor's goals and needs.

Example N°12: A mutual fund is composed of three types of government bonds: X, Y, and Z. The following table shows the bond market indices in two periods (N) and (N+1), along with the corresponding bond quantities traded in each company and their respective price movements (based on the reference price):

(n)	*Number of Bonds*	*PN+1*	*PN*	
400000	*120*	*118*	*X*	
550000	*130*	*125*	*Y*	*Index*
450000	*95*	*90*	*Z*	

Task:

1. *If the bond portfolio follows a fixed interest path that tracks the index movement, what strategy would be appropriate for this portfolio?*
2. *What is the ideal portfolio composition for the bond index in this scenario?*
3. *How does the index movement compare to other indexes? Does it follow an active or passive strategy?*

Solution :

1. Strategy for the Fixed Interest Portfolio:

Given the fixed interest path tracking the movement of the index, the Passive Strategy is most suitable. This is because the portfolio adjusts according to the market index without attempting to outperform it, i.e., the movements follow the market's general direction.

2. Ideal Portfolio Composition:

For an optimal portfolio, based on the provided information and considering a passive strategy, the portfolio would likely consist of a combination of X, Y, and Z bonds, weighted according to the bond quantities and their respective price movements.

Price Index=∑(Price×Number of Bonds)/ ∑(Number of Bonds)

Index	*X*	*Y*	*Z*
Price Index (PN)	*112.5*	*125*	*90*
Price Index (PN+1)	*116.2*	*130*	*95*
Change in Price	*+2*	*+5*	*+5*
Number of Bonds in N	*400000*	*550000*	*450000*
Number of Bonds in N+1	*350000*	*500000*	*400000*
Change in Number of Bonds	*-50000*	*-50000*	*-50000*
Percentage in N	*28.57%*	*39.29%*	*32.14%*
Percentage in N+1	*28%*	*40%*	*32%*

Since we are focusing on the portfolio composition based on the weights in N+1, the ideal portfolio composition should follow the weights of each bond type in N+1.

3. Active or Passive Strategy:

The portfolio in this exercise follows a passive strategy since it tracks the movements of the market index, without attempting to outperform it.

- **Bond Management Methods**:

  -Parallel Shift Strategy in Bond Portfolio Management : A parallel shift in the yield curve occurs when all interest rates across different maturities increase or decrease by the same amount. This means that the relationship between interest rates and maturities remains unchanged, but the entire yield curve shifts upward or downward in a parallel manner. A parallel shift is often caused by broad economic factors such as central bank interest rate decisions or shifts in overall inflation expectations.

  In practice, when a parallel shift occurs, investors typically adjust their bond portfolios based on the anticipated movement in interest rates. For instance, if interest rates are expected to rise uniformly across the yield curve, investors may seek to shorten the duration of their portfolios by moving into short-term bonds to mitigate the risk of falling bond prices. Conversely, if interest rates are expected to fall uniformly, extending the duration of a portfolio by investing in long-term bonds may offer higher yields and greater capital appreciation.

Application of the Parallel Shift Strategy:

1. Increased interest rates (Parallel shift upward):
   - Strategy: Reduce the exposure to long-duration bonds and increase investments in short-duration bonds.
   - Rationale: The price of long-duration bonds is more sensitive to interest rate changes, so a rise in interest rates would lead to a larger decrease in their value.
2. Decreased interest rates (Parallel shift downward):
   - Strategy: Increase exposure to long-duration bonds to benefit from price appreciation as rates decrease.
   - Rationale: Long-duration bonds increase in value when interest rates fall, allowing investors to lock in lower yields while gaining price appreciation.

-Non-Parallel Shift Strategy in Bond Portfolio Management: A non-parallel shift in the yield curve refers to a situation where the changes in interest rates are not uniform across different maturities. This can result in the yield curve steepening (where short-term interest rates rise less than long-term rates) or flattening (where short-term rates rise more than long-term rates). Non-parallel shifts are often driven by market expectations of inflation, growth, or changes in the central bank's monetary policy that are not expected to affect all maturities equally.

In this scenario, bond portfolio managers need to adopt a more dynamic approach to manage the risks and opportunities arising from these changes. A non-parallel shift requires careful analysis of the economic environment and interest rate forecasts. For example, if investors anticipate that short-term rates will rise significantly due to tightening monetary policy, they may choose to reduce exposure to short-term bonds and increase investments in long-term bonds, which may be less affected by the short-term rate movements. Alternatively, if the curve is expected to flatten, investors may adjust by holding bonds with intermediate maturities.
Application of the Non-Parallel Shift Strategy:

1. Steepening of the yield curve (long-term rates increase more than short-term rates):
   - Strategy: Increase exposure to long-term bonds while reducing holdings in short-term bonds.
   - Rationale: The increase in long-term rates might provide higher yields on long-term bonds, while short-term bonds may remain stable or see less pronounced yield increases.
2. Flattening of the yield curve (short-term rates increase more than long-term rates):
   - Strategy: Increase exposure to intermediate-term bonds that offer a balance between short-term and long-term maturities.
   - Rationale: Intermediate-term bonds will offer more favourable yield spreads relative to short-term bonds in a flattening yield curve environment.

– **Butterfly Shift:** This shift refers to larger changes in rates at intermediate maturities while rates at the short-term and long-term ends remain more stable or change slightly.

Strategy:

- Increase investment in medium-term bonds: Since the rate changes are expected to be larger at the medium term, investors can focus on bonds with medium-term maturities.
- Hold short- and long-term bonds: Because the rates at these maturities will change less, short- and long-term bonds could be more stable.

Example N°13: In the case of a significant rate increase at intermediate maturities, one might buy medium-term bonds while holding fewer short- and long-term bonds.

- **Twist Shift:** This shift occurs when short-term rates increase while long-term rates either stay stable or decrease.

Strategy:

- Reduce holdings in short-term bonds: Since the interest rates on short-term bonds will rise, the price of short-term bonds will be more adversely affected.
- Increase holdings in long-term bonds: If the long-term rates will be less impacted, increasing investments in long-term bonds could help take advantage of price stability.

Example N°14: If short-term rates rise significantly, you would sell short-term bonds and increase holdings in long-term bonds to benefit from stable rates.

- **Divergent Shift:** In this shift, short-term rates increase sharply, while long-term rates either rise slightly or remain lower. This leads to a wide gap between the short-term and long-term rates. Strategy:
    - Increase investment in long-term bonds: Since the short-term bonds are experiencing a sharp rise in rates, it may be more beneficial to focus

on long-term bonds for their relative price stability.

- Hedge using derivative instruments: Futures or options could be used to hedge against the risk of significant movements in the short-term bond sector.

Example N°15: If short-term rates rise significantly, reduce exposure to short-term bonds and increase investment in long-term bonds to benefit from their relative stability.

Figure 1: Representation of Interest Rate Changes Across Different Shift Types

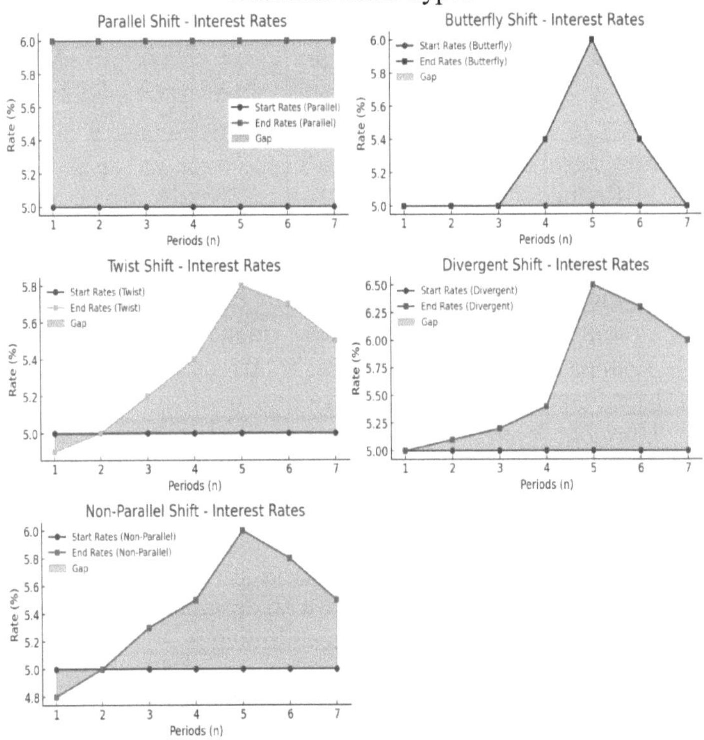

According to these changes in the structure, one can choose between three strategies:

- Ladder Strategy: This strategy involves spreading bond investments across multiple maturities to manage interest rate risk. The investor builds a portfolio consisting of bonds with different maturity dates, ranging from short-term to long-term. The aim is to provide consistent cash flow while reducing the impact of interest rate fluctuations on the portfolio. By ensuring bonds mature periodically, this strategy helps mitigate the risk of interest rate changes and provides liquidity.
- Barbell Strategy: In this strategy, a significant portion of the portfolio is allocated to both short-term and long-term bonds, while avoiding medium-term bonds. Typically, 60% of the portfolio is invested in short-term bonds, and the remaining 40% in long-term bonds. The goal is to balance the stability of short-term bonds with the potentially higher returns from long-term bonds, thus managing interest rate risk. The barbell strategy provides a mix of predictable returns from short-term bonds and higher yields from long-term bonds.
- Bullet Strategy: This strategy focuses on bonds with a single maturity date or creates a bond ladder centred around one specific date. The investor concentrates their portfolio on bonds that mature simultaneously, allowing for better management of interest rate expectations and capital returns at that maturity point. This approach enables more precise forecasting in favourable market conditions, especially when interest rates are expected to remain stable.
- Buy and Hold Strategy: The investor purchases bonds and holds them until maturity, avoiding frequent

adjustments to the portfolio. This strategy is based on the assumption that the market will continue to generate reasonable returns over time without the need for active management. It is straightforward, reduces transaction costs, and is ideal for investors seeking stable, long-term returns without continuous portfolio changes.

Example N° 16: A mutual fund is composed of three categories of bonds: short-term bonds, medium-term bonds, and long-term bonds. The first group of bonds includes A, B, C, and D bonds. The second group is composed of E, F, and G bonds. The bonds have the following characteristics:

Bonds	*A*	*B*	*C*	*D*	*E*	*F*	*G*
Term	*Short*	*Short*	*Medium*	*Medium*	*Long*	*Long*	*Long*
Years to Maturity	*1*	*3*	*5*	*7*	*10*	*15*	*20*
Value (in thousands)	*500*	*300*	*200*	*400*	*100*	*50*	*25*

Task: What strategy would be appropriate for constructing the portfolio (Barbell – Ladder – Bullet)? Explain the reasoning for each strategy.

Solution:

-Portfolio Construction for Barbell Strategy:

- *Short-term bonds (A + B): 60% × (500 + 300) = 480*
- *Long-term bonds (F + G): 40% × (50 + 25) = 30*

Bonds	*A*	*B*	*F*	*G*
Value (in thousands)	*480*	*480*	*30*	*-*
% of Total Portfolio	*60%*	*60%*	*40%*	*-*

-Ladder Strategy: Allocate bonds across all three categories: short-term (A, B), medium-term (C, D), and long-term (E, F, G).

Bonds	*A*	*B*	*C*	*D*	*E*	*F*	*G*

Value (in thousands)	*500*	*300*	*200*	*400*	*100*	*50*	*25*
% of Total Portfolio	*25%*	*15%*	*10%*	*20%*	*5%*	*2.5%*	*1.25%*

-Portfolio Construction for Bullet Strategy: Focus on bonds with the same or similar maturity dates. Here, we will combine bonds with maturities of 1 year (A) and 3 years (B) as they are close enough for this strategy.

Bonds	*A*	*B*
Value (in thousands)	*500*	*300*
% of Total Portfolio	*50%*	*50%*

Example N° 17: Given the following data on interest rates across different maturities:

n	*7*	*6*	*5*	*4*	*3*	*2*	*1*
Starting Rate	*9.0*	*8.5*	*8.0*	*7.5*	*7.0*	*6.5*	*6.0*
Change in Rate	*2.5*	*2.3*	*2.1*	*2.0*	*2.3*	*2.5*	*2.7*

Tasks:

1. *Plot the Movement of Interest Rates:*
   - *Using the given data, plot the starting rates and ending rates over the periods of maturities.*
   - *Identify if the changes occur in a parallel or non-parallel manner.*
2. *Determine the Type of Shift in the Yield Curve:*
   - *Since the changes in rates across the periods are not equal, determine whether the shift is parallel or non-parallel.*
3. *Identify Suitable Portfolio Management Strategies:*
   - *If the shift is parallel, what strategy would you employ to reduce the impact of the changes in interest rates on the portfolio?*
   - *If the shift is non-parallel, how would you adjust your investments across short-term and long-term bonds?*

4. Represent the Values When All Rates Are Equal:

- *Assume all rates are equal across the maturities (i.e. $a_1=a_2=a_3=a_4=a_5=a_6=a_7$*
- *What would the change in the rates be if all values were the same?*

Solution:

n	7	6	5	4	3	2	1
Starting Rate	9.0	8.5	8.0	7.5	7.0	6.5	6.0
Change in Rate	2.5	2.3	2.1	2.0	2.3	2.5	2.7
Ending Rate	6.5	6.2	6.0	5.5	4.7	4.0	3.3

1. Plotting the Movement of Interest Rates:

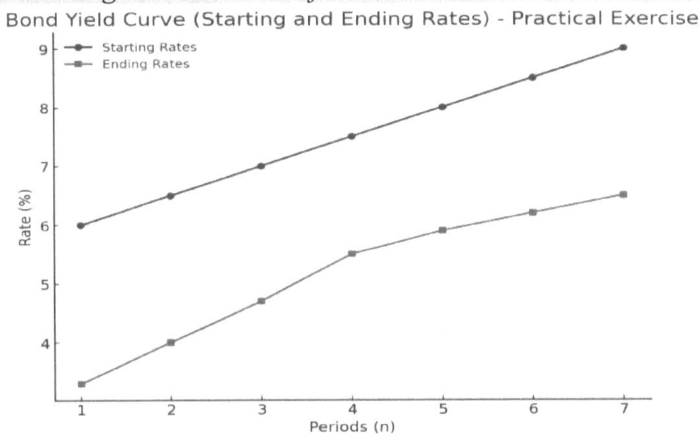

2. Determine the Type of Shift: The changes in rates across the maturities are not uniform, meaning that the rate changes differ between short-term and long-term maturities. This indicates a non-parallel shift in the yield curve.

3. Portfolio Management Strategies:

- *Parallel Shift: If the shift were parallel, meaning all rates change by the same amount, the appropriate strategy would be to adjust the duration of the portfolio. This involves either shortening the duration (selling long-term bonds and buying short-term ones) when rates are expected to rise or lengthening the duration (buying long-term bonds) when rates are expected to fall.*

- *Non-Parallel Shift: Since the shift is non-parallel, the strategy would depend on which maturities are expected to experience greater changes:*
    - *If rates are expected to increase on the short end (short-term bonds), reduce holdings in short-term bonds and possibly increase holdings in long-term bonds.*
    - *Conversely, if the increase is expected on the long end, focus investments on short-term bonds and adjust long-term holdings accordingly.*

4. Representing the Values When All Rates Are Equal: If all the rates were equal, there would be no change between the starting and ending rates (i.e., the change would be zero). This means the yield curve would be flat, and no adjustments would be required in response to interest rate changes.

6.3.3 Tactical Asset Allocation Strategy: This strategy revolves around the allocation of assets in a portfolio to achieve a balance between returns and risks. The key focus is on adjusting the proportions of different asset classes, such as stocks, bonds, and cash, based on market conditions and the investor's goals. The success of this strategy is largely dependent on the ability to predict overall market movements (i.e., macroeconomic trends, interest rates, or economic indicators), rather than focusing on the performance of individual companies or securities. Portfolio managers often use technical and quantitative analysis to guide their decisions, which includes examining price trends, patterns, and economic factors that may influence the market as a whole.

6.3.4 Insured Asset Allocation Strategy: This strategy aims to protect the investor's capital by mitigating potential losses during unfavorable market conditions. It involves adjusting the allocation of investments by moving funds between higher-risk assets, like stocks, and low-risk, safer assets, such as risk-free bonds. The portfolio manager monitors market fluctuations and shifts the allocation based on anticipated changes in market conditions. The goal is to safeguard the portfolio from significant losses while still pursuing growth by maintaining a diversified investment approach.

6.4 Portfolio Hedging Strategies

Hedging in a portfolio refers to the risk management strategy used to offset potential losses in investments by taking opposing positions. This practice involves dealing with risk through various means such as risk avoidance, risk reduction, or risk transfer. Hedging can be achieved via insurance, diversification (natural hedging), and the use of derivatives.

A. Stop-Loss Strategy: The stop-loss strategy is one of the simplest methods of hedging. It involves constructing a portfolio with a stock index and risk-free assets, such as government bonds. The stop-loss is designed to secure the portfolio value composed of stocks. This strategy relies on selling stocks when their value approaches the minimum threshold and buying bonds when stock values drop below that threshold. Below is an example illustrating this strategy:

Example N°18: Consider a period with 5 intervals. The minimum value at time T equals 5. Stock price = 100, and the interest rate for 5 periods is 2%. The minimum value, FT, is defined at time $T \leq T$.

Period	*Stocks*	*Government Bonds*	*Minimum Value*	*Portfolio Value*
0	*100*	*0*	*100*	*100*

1	*105*	*0*	*100.40*	*105*
2	*98*	*98*	*98.82*	*98*
3	*98.39*	*0*	*99.21*	*98.39*
4	*98.78*	*0*	*99.60*	*102.65*
5	*102.65*	*0*	*100*	*106*

In this table, the portfolio manager sells the stock index when its value intersects with the minimum value and buys when the stock price is higher than the minimum value. Although this strategy works in theory, it has limitations such as:

- *It does not account for transaction costs.*
- *It works effectively only when there are two market directions. When stock prices increase, they should remain high in subsequent periods.*
- *Capital protection via switching between stocks and bonds cannot be executed perfectly when the portfolio value is close to the minimum threshold.*

B . Cushion Strategy (CPPI): The Cushion Strategy was created by Perlo in 1986 and developed by Black and Jones in 1987. It involves ensuring a certain percentage of the portfolio's capital by investing in bonds, with the remaining portion allocated to stocks. The strategy guarantees a portion of the capital, such as 95%, while leaving 5% in stocks. The gap between the portfolio's value and its minimum is the capital being protected. This strategy also considers potential losses in the stock market on 100% a daily basis.

Example N°19: We take a portfolio with an initial value of 100, and we aim to secure 95% of its capital through bonds, with the remaining 5% invested in stocks. This value is referred to as the cushion.

The difference between the portfolio value and the minimum value represents the capital we are trying to protect; this strategy assumes a 100% loss in the stock market in one day.

Thus, the portfolio (the cushion value) may face the maximum potential loss. To estimate potential losses or sensitivity index, it is traditional to include the time factor (T), which can be estimated between 30 and 50 years. Therefore, T defines the acceptable loss probability in the cushion strategy. This probability is: $\frac{1}{252*T}$

252: the number of trading days in a year.

Let's assume the probability of loss is 15% for every T = 50, meaning the market can lose 15% rather than 100%, and similarly for the portfolio or any other portfolio.

Thus, we can invest where: $33.35 \square \frac{100}{15} \times 5$ the sensitivity index is denoted as: $\frac{100}{15}$

"m" is the multiplier, and if we invest 33.35, the maximum loss will be 5, and the minimum value will be surpassed every 50 years.

The term "e" in stocks is the multiplier of the cushion strategy. $e = c \times m$

- e: the value of investment in stocks,
- c: the cushion capital,
- m: the multiplier.

The remaining amount will be invested in bonds, i.e., 66.65. Thus, c always changes with the minimum value, and the value invested in stocks must always equal e to maintain balance. Typically, the multiplier value is set at 10%, where the lower the multiplier, the lower the protection

C. Hedging Using Futures Contracts: Futures contracts are used as a means of hedging, where an investor may have a long-term position and is thus exposed to the risks of price fluctuations of the asset. To reduce these risks, the investor seeks to take a short-term position in the futures market by contracting to sell the asset, which is referred to as Short Hedging. On the other hand, if the investor needs an asset in the future, they can take a long-term position by contracting to purchase the asset through the futures market, known as Long Hedging.

Futures contracts are also used on stock market indices (as a benchmark) to hedge a portfolio of stocks against price volatility. Several scenarios are important, such as:

- Let p be the current value of the portfolio.
- A represents the value of the stock portfolio that forms the index (the benchmark).

- **In the case where the hedged stock portfolio has the same composition as the index**:

$$h^* = P\left(\theta_s / \theta_F\right) \qquad (19)$$

Where:

- D_S: Price changes during the coverage period.
- D_F: Price changes during the coverage period.
- θ_S: Standard deviation of DS.
- θ_F: Standard deviation of DF.
- P: The correlation between DS and DF.
- R^*: The coverage ratio that reduces the risk on the position to be hedged.

Thus, the minimum coverage ratio = 1.
For the minimum contracts:

$$N^* = h^*\left(N_a / \varphi_F\right) \qquad (20)$$

- N^*: The number of minimum positions required for the hedge.
- N_a: The size of the asset to be covered (in units).
- Q_f: The size of a single futures contract (in units).

In this case, the optimal number of contracts for coverage is calculated.

$$N^* = P/A \qquad (21)$$

Example N°20: Suppose we have a stock portfolio that matches the CAC40 composition with a value of 3 million euros, and the futures contract on this index is worth €10 multiplied by the index value. If the market index price is 3000 points, the optimal number of contracts for coverage would be:

$$N^* = \frac{3.000.000}{30.000} = 100 \begin{cases} €3.000.000 : p \\ €30.000 = 10 \times 3000 : A \end{cases}$$

Thus, a short position on 100 futures contracts is required to hedge the portfolio.

- ***If the portfolio to be hedged has a different composition from the index, we use the portfolio's β to determine the optimal number of contracts for coverage (MDAF).***

$$N^* = \beta \frac{P}{A} \qquad (22)$$

Note:

- *β > 1: Portfolio changes increase and rise with the index changes.*
- *β < 1: Portfolio changes decrease with the index changes.*

Example N°21: The CAC price is 3000 points = ST0.

- *The portfolio value is €1,600,000.*
- *The annual government bond yield is 5% (risk-free rate).*
- *The index yield is 2%.*
- *Portfolio β = 1.5.*

Each CAC40 futures contract is based on the index value × 10€. We want coverage for 3 months. The futures contracts on the CAC40 index last for 4 months, and their price is 3030.15 (K0) points.

The optimal number of contracts for coverage is calculated

$N^* = 1.5 \frac{1.600.000}{30.000} = 80$, *and thus a short position on 80 CAC40 futures contracts is required.*

If the index price drops to 2700 (ST_1) after three months, and the futures price becomes 2706.75 (K1), the profits on the contracts will be:

- *The portfolio yield = Risk-free rate + β (index rate – risk-free rate).*
- *Loss on the index = 3000 – 2700, which is a 10% drop in value.*
- *The yield of the tri-index is 0.5% (note it is 2% annually). Thus, the final loss on the index is: -10 + 0.5 = -9.5 over the quarter.*
- *The risk-free rate is 5% annually, which is 1.25% in the quarter.*
- *Therefore, the expected portfolio yield is:* $\%14.875 - = 1.25 + \left[(1.25 - 9.25 -) \times 1.5 \right]$

Expected portfolio value $[0.14875 - 1] \times 1.600.000$ = €1.362.000

The final result of the operation: the results on the contracts + the expected portfolio value = 1,362,000 + 265,181 = 1,627,181€.

- **Changing β for a Stock Portfolio:** Futures contracts are used to adjust β without converting it to 0.

In general, to change β from a specific value to *β where β < *β, a short position on futures contracts equal to:

$$N^* = (\beta - \beta^*) . \frac{P}{A} \tag{23}$$

In the case where *β < β, a long position on the required number of futures contracts should be taken:

$$N^{*} = (\beta^{*} - \beta).\frac{P}{A} \qquad (24)$$

- **Sliding Hedge (Couverture glissante):** In some cases, the required coverage exceeds the life of the futures contracts traded on the market. In this case, the hedge trader divides and shifts the risk from time to time.

  An economic operator expects to receive a cash value on date T and wants to hedge against price fluctuations. They can use n consecutive futures contracts as follows:

Short position on contract 1

↓

Close out contract 1 at T_l

↓

Short position on contract 2

↓

Closc out contraet $n = 1$ at T_l Short position on contract n

Rolling hedging

D. Option-Based Hedging Strategy (OBPI): Options are one of the most important financial tools in hedging strategies, as they provide investors with the right, but not the obligation, to buy or sell an asset at a predetermined price in the future. These instruments are used to hedge against risks arising from price fluctuations. Below is an explanation of the simple options hedging strategies:

- **Hedging with a Call Option:** This strategy allows the investor to hedge against the risks associated with potential price increases in the future. A call option is purchased on the assets owned by the investor, granting them the right to buy the asset at a specified price in the future.

Example N°22: Assume a portfolio manager holds stocks valued at 12 dinars. Given the expectation that the stock price will rise in the future, but anticipating a temporary decline in price due to certain economic factors, the manager purchases a call option with an exercise price of 10 dinars and a premium of 5 dinars.

If the price rises above 10 dinars at the exercise date, the manager can purchase the stock at the lower exercise price and sell it at the higher market price. If the price falls below 10 dinars, the premium paid is lost.

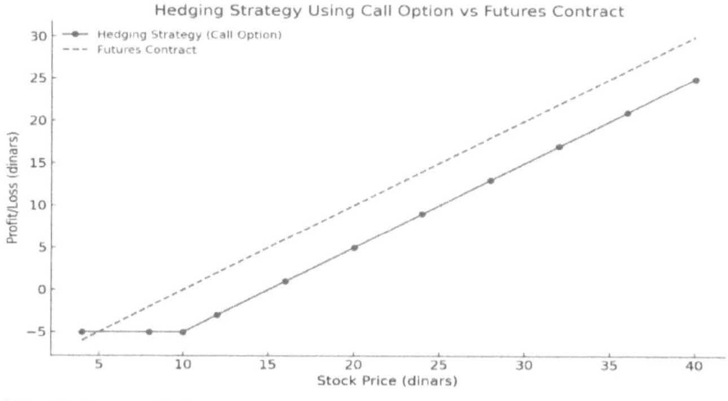

- **Hedging with a Put Option :** This strategy allows the investor to protect their portfolio against potential price declines. By purchasing a put option, the investor secures the right to sell the asset at a predetermined price in the future.

Example N°23: If the portfolio manager holds 1000 shares, each priced at 73 euros, and expects a decrease in value, they may purchase 100 put option contracts with an exercise price of 65 euros and a premium of 2.5 euros per share. If the price falls below 65 euros, the investor can sell the shares at the exercise price (65 euros), effectively protecting against losses. If the price remains above 65 euros, the option will not be exercised, but the premium paid will be lost.

Solution : 10 shares × 65 euros = 2500 euros (premium paid)

If the strike price is 65 euros per share, the investor pays: x/2500

Cost: The cost of this strategy is 2500 euros, ensuring the investor can sell their shares at a price lower than 65 euros during the contract period.

In the case where the stock price falls below 65 euros: The investor can sell their shares, and the final outcome would be as follows: 62500 = 2500 × 65 − 1000

In the case where the stock price remains above 65 euros: The investor does not sell their shares, and their value exceeds 62500 euros

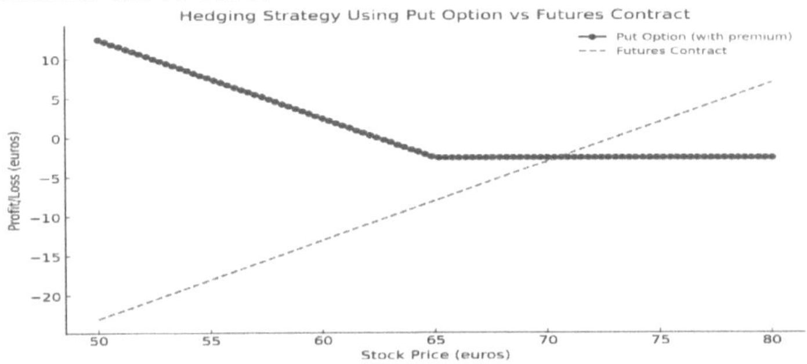

- **Hedging with a Straddle Option:** This strategy involves purchasing both a call option and a put option for the same asset at the same time. It is used when the investor expects significant price fluctuations but cannot predict the direction of the price change (either up or down).
- **Bullish Option Strategy (Step)**: This contract involves purchasing "two call options" and "one put option," typically when the investor believes that the market will trend upwards, although not being fully certain. The investor may also be wary of potential price fluctuations that might go against their favour. Therefore, the strategy

is to purchase a double option to protect against risks and take advantage of their forecast by increasing the buying rights over the selling rights.

- **Bearish Option Strategy (Strip):**This is the reverse of the previous strategy and is known as the "bearish option strategy" or "put option." If the investor's expectations lean more towards a decline in prices than an increase, they may buy two put options and one call option. The contract is executed based on what benefits the investor, depending on the price levels. If prices rise, the call option is exercised, whereas if prices fall, the two put options are exercised, allowing the investor to realise profits accordingly.

6.5 Portfolio Management Decisions

Portfolio management decisions are primarily based on the portfolio manager's expertise and experience in applying portfolio theory. The key decisions made include:

A. Investment Mix Selection (Asset Allocation and Reallocation Decision): The first step in portfolio management involves determining the percentage of the total assets to be allocated for investment in stocks, while the remaining portion is held in highly liquid assets. This important decision is made based on the portfolio manager's expectations regarding the stock market. If the manager believes the market will rise in the upcoming period, they will increase the stock allocation to 100% of the portfolio. Conversely, if the manager expects the market to decline, they may shift some investments into government bonds to avoid potential losses. The goal of this optimal allocation is:

- Achieving the highest return at a certain level of risk.
- Minimising risk to the lowest possible level.

This problem can be formulated mathematically using an objective function, as follows:

$$min\delta_P^2 = \sum_{i=1}^{n}\sum_{j=1}^{n} w_i \ w_j \, \delta_{ij} \tag{25}$$

Where:

- n: Total number of investments.
- δ_P^2: The variance of the portfolio to minimise risk.
- W_i: *and* W_j: are the weights of the assets in the portfolio.
- δ_{ij}: The covariance between the returns of asset i and asset j.

With the constraint of a specific return level, this equation can be solved using simplex software.

$$\sum_{i=1}^{n} W_i = 1 \tag{26}$$

$$\sum_{i=1}^{n} W_i \, E_i = E^* \tag{27}$$

Equation N°26 is a constraint for portfolio weights. It ensures that the sum of all asset weights w1,w2,…,wn in the portfolio must equal 1, meaning the entire capital is allocated among the assets.

Equation N°27 represents the expected return of the portfolio, where:

- Ei is the expected return of asset i,
- Wi is the weight of asset i,
- E^* is the target expected return of the entire portfolio.

This equation expresses the fact that the weighted sum of the expected returns of the individual assets must equal the overall expected return of the portfolio.

B. Diversification Decision: Diversification refers to the manager's decision to form a portfolio composition that can reduce the risk exposure to portfolio returns. There are several different principles for portfolio construction or diversification, with the most important ones being:

- **Horizontal Diversification**: This involves including securities of the same type in the portfolio. It can be a broad diversification, such as investing in stocks from the same branch or sector, or stocks from different sectors (e.g., investing in bank stocks, cement company stocks, and phosphate company stocks). This type of diversification reduces investment risks because the correlation between the banking sector and the industrial sector is negative.
- **Vertical Diversification:** This involves investing in different types of securities, such as stocks, bonds, or other financial instruments like fixed-income securities or variable-income securities. This type of diversification achieves the goal of reducing risks because even though the investment will be in homogeneous instruments with similar characteristics, the correlation between them can be negative, reducing the risk further. Vertical diversification also protects from market risks or economic changes.
- **Geographical Diversification (International Diversification):** This involves investing in several different geographical sectors. Since international financial markets, especially in developed countries, are linked, an investor can diversify in markets like France or the USA, which would be less risky than a portfolio consisting only of French stocks.
- **Issuer Diversification:** Issuer diversification involves not allocating the portfolio's funds to securities issued by a single entity. There are two common methods in this regard:
  - **Simple Diversification**: This approach is based on the basic idea that the more diversified the investments in

the portfolio, the lower the risks. For example, a portfolio of bonds issued by three different institutions would expose the investor to lower risk compared to a portfolio of bonds issued by just two institutions. Studies have shown that simple diversification ensures the elimination of most idiosyncratic (specific) risks, or systematic risks.

The study conducted by Avatzouarch indicates that the simple diversification method ensures the elimination of most of the idiosyncratic risks, i.e., the systematic risks. However, it must be taken into account that excessive diversification of the portfolio components may have adverse effects, the most important of which are:

- Difficulty in managing the portfolio, especially when the number of issuers of financial instruments increases, as this requires continuous analysis of the financial position of the issuing institutions.
- High costs for seeking new investments.
- Making incorrect investment decisions, as excessive diversification may lead the management to invest in financial instruments that generate returns that do not align with the associated risks.
- Increased average transaction costs, as excessive diversification leads to higher investment acquisition costs.

– **Markowitz Diversification**: Unlike simple diversification, which involves random selection of portfolio investments, Markowitz's approach requires careful selection based on the correlation (correlation coefficient) between the returns of the assets. When there is a positive correlation between the returns of investments in a portfolio, the risks are greater than when the returns are independent (negative correlation). Markowitz concluded that the lower the correlation between individual investment returns, the lower the risks faced by the portfolio's returns.

The correlation coefficient is calculated for two stocks, for example.

$$R = \frac{COV(R_A + R_B)}{\delta(R_A) + \delta(R_B)} \tag{28}$$

It should be noted that this method of diversification may not only succeed in eliminating idiosyncratic risks, but also in reducing part of the systematic risks.

- **Maturity Date Diversification:** The portfolio manager faces the risk of interest rate fluctuations, especially if the portfolio consists of bonds. This price fluctuation affects short-term bonds more than long-term bonds, as the latter tend to be more stable. The dilemma faced by the portfolio manager regarding the allocation of funds between long-term and short-term bonds can be overcome through a maturity ladder diversification strategy. There are two methods:
  - **Aggressive Approach**: In this approach, the portfolio manager constantly shifts from short-term bonds to long-term bonds depending on market conditions. If interest rates are expected to rise, the manager would sell long-term bonds and use the proceeds to buy short-term bonds. If interest rates are predicted to decline, the manager would take advantage of this opportunity.
  - **Ladder Maturity Structure**: This strategy involves distributing the portfolio's allocations across investments with staggered maturity dates. The portfolio manager establishes a structure for maturity dates and ensures investments are spread

over a range of maturities, helping with liquidity management and protecting against declines in the market value of investments.

- **Focusing on Short-term and Long-term Investments**: The approach of focusing on both short-term and long-term investments involves excluding medium-term securities, typically those with maturities between 3 and 7 years. A portfolio is then constructed with short-term investments (less than 3 years) and long-term investments (7 to 10 years). The rationale behind this approach is that short-term investments contribute to meeting liquidity requirements, while long-term investments address profitability needs. Medium-term investments, on the other hand, lie in between. The allocation of the portfolio is based on the economic situation (recession or boom) and the direction of interest rates

C. Decision on Financial Instruments Selection: After selecting the financial instruments for the portfolio, it is essential to choose the appropriate financial tools that align with the portfolio's objectives. This decision is based on various factors, including asset evaluation and the foundation for selecting and including them in the portfolio. A thorough analytical study (both technical and fundamental analysis) is required to understand the nature of the company issuing the instruments.

D. Investment Timing Decision: The decision of when to buy or sell is a critical one in portfolio management. The principle of "when to buy" depends on basic concepts that must be adhered to when making purchases. To answer this question, technical factors must be analysed, such as whether the price trend is moving upwards or downwards, and determining the position of the second peak relative to the first. The portfolio manager should also assess the market trend and evaluate the likelihood of price improvements, as well as understanding whether the market is at the peak of an upward trend or heading into a continuous decline. Furthermore, the manager must evaluate how far the stock price is from its true value.

6.6 Portfolio Management Policies

- **Risk Policy or Aggressive Policy**: This policy is characterised by the rapid generation of exceptional capital gains and takes advantage of the portfolio management's ability to exploit discrepancies between the market value of selected financial instruments and their true or fair value. This policy is associated with high risk due to the economic variables that affect the chosen instruments within the portfolio.
- **Defensive Policy (Conservative Policy)**: This is the policy adopted by the portfolio management to cater to the preferences of conservative investors, prioritising security over returns. Portfolio management relies on selecting fixed or semi-fixed income investment tools, which is why such portfolios are referred to as income portfolios. The management gives considerable importance to low-risk investment tools when they participate in capital. This policy may be chosen when there are economic indicators suggesting the economy is heading towards recession or economic downturn.
- **Balanced Offensive-Defensive Policy**: This policy blends both conservatism and risk, and is widely used by most portfolio managers as it aligns with the desires of mature investors who focus on achieving relative stability in returns and obtaining reasonable profits with acceptable risks. Thus, the portfolio policy will be based on dividing the capital into two sections:
  - Investment in high-return instruments.

- Investment in fixed-income instruments.

6.7 Steps in Portfolio Management

The following represents the process of portfolio management:

Step 1" Strategic Plan":

- Goal Setting: Define the portfolio's objectives, including target returns, acceptable risk levels, and other specific goals such as income generation or capital appreciation.
- KPI Definition: Establish Key Performance Indicators (KPIs) to track progress and assess the portfolio's performance towards meeting its objectives.
- Capacity Definition: Identify the portfolio's capacity for risk (how much risk the investor is willing to accept) and the available investment resources (capital and liquidity available for investment).

Step 2" Alignment Process":

- Component Identification: Identify the individual assets or securities that will form the portfolio (stocks, bonds, etc.).
- Categorisation of Components: Classify these assets according to their type (e.g., equity, debt, real estate).
- Evaluation of Components: Assess each asset based on performance metrics such as historical returns, risk, liquidity, and potential for future growth.
- Selection of Components: Choose the securities that meet the portfolio's objectives, risk profile, and asset allocation strategy.
- Prioritisation of Components: Prioritise the assets based on expected returns and risk levels, focusing on those that align with the portfolio's goals.
- Development of Risk Responses: Develop strategies to manage the identified risks in the portfolio, including

hedging strategies, diversification, and setting stop-loss levels.

- Portfolio Balancing: Ensure the portfolio is balanced with the appropriate mix of assets to meet the desired risk-return trade-off.
- Communication of Adjustments: Inform relevant stakeholders about changes made to the portfolio and the reasons for these adjustments.
- Authorisation of Components: Ensure that all selected components comply with regulatory standards and internal approval processes

Step 3" Monitoring and Control Processes":

- Monitor Portfolio Risks: Continuously monitor the portfolio for any emerging risks (market volatility, liquidity issues, etc.) that may affect performance.
- Portfolio Performance Review and Reporting: Regularly assess how the portfolio is performing relative to the pre-set objectives and KPIs, and make adjustments as necessary.
- Monitor Changes in Business Strategy: Ensure the portfolio adapts to any significant changes in the business or economic environment that could impact its performance (e.g., market downturns, new regulations, geopolitical events).

Step 4" Component Execution and Reporting":

- Execution of Portfolio Adjustments: Make necessary changes to the portfolio based on performance reviews and updated market information (e.g., rebalancing assets, changing allocations).
- Periodic Reporting: Provide stakeholders with regular updates on the portfolio's status, performance, and any required changes or adjustments, ensuring transparency.

Step 5" Risk Management and Diversification":

- Identify Risks: Assess various types of risks (market risk, liquidity risk, operational risk, etc.) that could affect portfolio performance.
- Diversify the Portfolio: Implement diversification strategies (horizontal, vertical, geographical) to spread risk and reduce the potential impact of any one asset's poor performance.
- Asset Allocation: Allocate the portfolio's capital to various asset classes (stocks, bonds, real estate, etc.) to balance risk and reward according to the investor's goals and risk tolerance.
- Ensure Liquidity: Ensure that assets can be quickly converted into cash (or liquidated) without significant loss of value, meeting any potential cash flow requirements or investor withdrawal needs.

Step 6 "Performance Evaluation":

- Evaluate Portfolio Performance: Measure the portfolio's success against the predefined KPIs and target objectives (e.g., achieving a certain rate of return, staying within a certain risk tolerance).
- Risk and Return Analysis: Regularly analyse the portfolio's risk-adjusted returns (e.g., Sharpe ratio, alpha) to ensure the portfolio is performing well within the expected risk parameters.
- Adjust Portfolio Strategy: If the performance analysis reveals any gaps or underperformance, adjust the portfolio's strategy to optimise returns, reduce risks, or better align with market conditions and investor goals.

6.8 Key Factors to Consider in Portfolio Management

- **Market Conditions:** Economic indicators such as inflation rates, interest rates, and overall market trends can heavily influence portfolio performance.

- **Risk Tolerance:** The portfolio manager must understand and adjust to the investor's ability to bear risk and tailor the portfolio accordingly.
- **Liquidity Needs:** The ability to quickly liquidate investments without incurring major losses is crucial for maintaining flexibility.
- **Investment Horizon:** The time frame for investment plays a critical role in determining the risk profile and asset allocation.
- **Diversification:** Proper diversification helps mitigate risks by spreading investments across various assets and markets.

Chapter Seven
Financial Portfolio Models

Chapter Seven: Financial Portfolio Models

This chapter delves into the key financial portfolio models that assist investors in strategically allocating their assets, aiming to optimise returns while managing risk. It covers fundamental models such as the Efficient Portfolio, CAPM, SML, and APT, highlighting their theoretical foundations and practical implications in portfolio management.

7.1 Efficient and Optimal Portfolios

- **Efficient portfolio**: This refers to portfolios that offer the highest expected return for a given level of risk, or those that achieve the lowest possible risk for a specific expected return level. The following figure illustrates this concept.

Figure N°1: Efficient Investment Curve

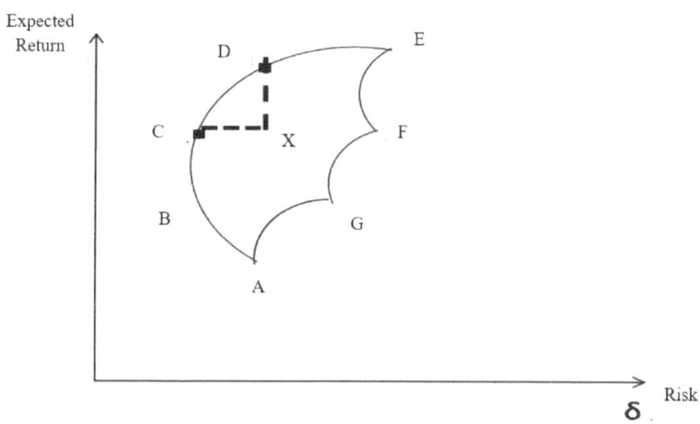

The curve "A B C D E" represents the set of efficient portfolios, with no portfolios located on the left side. Portfolios on the right side are inefficient because other portfolios can provide higher returns for the same level of risk, or they expose the investor to lower levels of risk for the same expected return.

To identify the portfolio that aligns with the investor's interests (the optimal portfolio), it is essential to understand the investor's risk preference, which is a trade-off function between return and risk. This function is based on the economic concept of indifference curves. The following figure illustrates this for Mr. (A) and Mr. (B). It can be observed that for Mr. (A), he is indifferent between a portfolio that offers a 40% return with no risk and a portfolio with a 14% return at a 3.8% risk level. On the other hand, Mr. (B) is indifferent between a portfolio that gives him an 8% return with a 7% risk level. Figure 2 demonstrates this scenario.

Figure N° 2: Indifference Curves for Risk and Expected Return

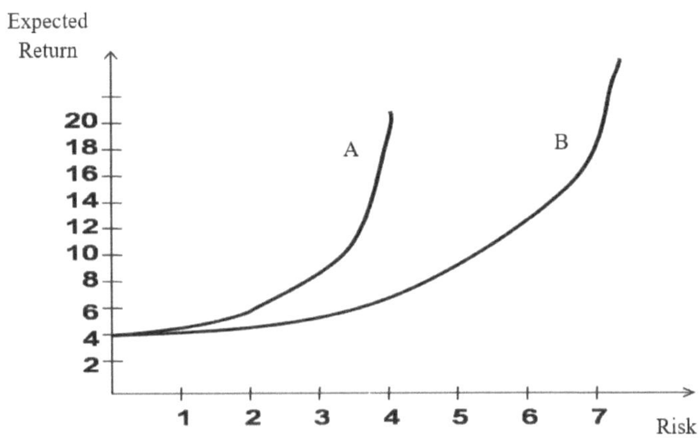

Example N° 24: You are provided with the following data for three assets. Calculate the covariance and variance, and then build an efficient portfolio consisting of 50% of Asset 1 and

50% of Asset 2. Calculate the expected return and standard deviation of the portfolio.

Asset	Expected Return (%)	Standard Deviation (%)	Correlation with Asset 1	Correlation with Asset 2	Correlation with Asset 3
Asset 1	8%	10%	1	0.4	0.3
Asset 2	12%	15%	0.4	1	0.5
Asset 3	10%	12%	0.3	0.5	1

Solution

We calculate the covariance between each pair of assets using the following formula:

$$Cov(i,j)=\rho(i,j)\cdot\sigma(i)\cdot\sigma(j)$$

where:

- $\rho(i,j)$ *is the correlation coefficient.*
- $\sigma(i)$ *and* $\sigma(j)$ *are the standard deviations of assets iand j.*

	Asset 1	Asset 2	Asset 3
Asset 1	$10\%^2=0.01$	$0.4\times 10\%\times 15\%=0.6\%$	$0.3\times 10\%\times 12\%=0.36\%$
Asset 2	$0.4\times 10\%\times 15\%=0.6\%$	$15\%^2=0.0225$	$0.5\times 15\%\times 12\%=0.9\%$
Asset 3	$0.3\times 10\%\times 12\%=0.36\%$	$0.5\times 15\%\times 12\%=0.9\%$	$12\%^2=0.0144$

Calculate the Efficient Portfolio (50% of Asset 1 and 50% of Asset 2)

where:

- $w_1=0.5$ $w_2=0.5$
- $\sigma_1=10\%$, $\sigma_2=15\%$
- Cov(1,2)=0.006

$\sigma_{p2}=w_{12}\cdot\sigma_{12}+w_{22}\cdot\sigma_{22}+2\cdot w_1\cdot w_2\cdot Cov(1,2)$

$\sigma_{p2}=(0.5)^2\cdot(0.10)^2+(0.5)^2\cdot(0.15)^2+2\cdot(0.5)\cdot(0.5)\cdot=0.1055$

The expected return of the portfolio is calculated as:
$E(R_p)=w_1 \cdot E(R_1)+w_2 \cdot E(R_2)E(R\_p)$
E(Rp)= 0.5·8%+0.5·12%=4%+6%=10%
where:

- $E(R_1)$=8%, $E(R_2)$=12%,

Variable	Value
Expected Return	10%
Standard Deviation	10.55%

- **The optimal portfolio:** The optimal portfolio is the point of tangency between the set of efficient portfolios and the indifference curve, and this tangency point represents the highest level of satisfaction that an investor can achieve.

The problem of portfolio management is to construct the optimal portfolio, which lies at the best point on the indifference curve. By identifying the efficient frontier along with the various indifference curves, it becomes easier to choose the securities and make decisions regarding their selection and the amount of money to be invested, as illustrated in Figure 3. The suitable portfolio is represented by point D on the indifference curve L2 and L4.

Figure N° 3: Selection of the Optimal Portfolio

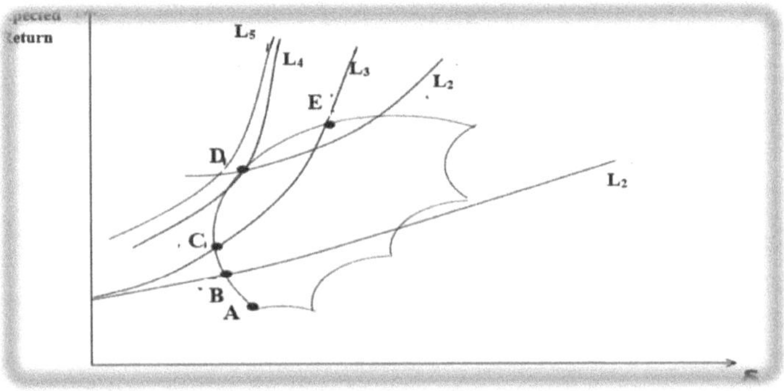

Example N° 25: Given the following data for four assets, build a portfolio consisting of 30% of Asset 1, 30% of Asset 2, and 40% of Asset 3. Calculate the expected return and standard deviation of this portfolio. Then, assume the investor has a moderate risk preference, and identify the optimal portfolio using indifference curves with a maximum risk of 15%.

Asset	*ER %*	*σ (%)*	ρ *A 1*	ρ *A 2*	ρ *A 3*	ρ *A 4*
Asset 1	*10%*	*12%*	*1*	*0.6*	*0.5*	*0.4*
Asset 2	*8%*	*10%*	*0.6*	*1*	*0.7*	*0.5*
Asset 3	*12%*	*18%*	*0.5*	*0.7*	*1*	*0.6*
Asset 4	*9%*	*14%*	*0.4*	*0.5*	*0.6*	*1*

Solution: We calculate the covariance between each pair of assets using the same formula:

$Cov(i,j)=\rho_{(i,j)}\cdot\sigma(_i)\cdot\sigma(_j)$

Covariance and Variance Matrix

	Asset 1	*Asset 2*	*Asset 3*	*Asset 4*
Asset 1	*0.0100*	*0.0072*	*0.0060*	*0.0050*
Asset 2	*0.0072*	*0.0100*	*0.0084*	*0.0060*
Asset 3	*0.0060*	*0.0084*	*0.0324*	*0.0084*
Asset 4	*0.0050*	*0.0060*	*0.0084*	*0.0196*

Given the portfolio weights of 30% for Asset 1, 30% for Asset 2, and 40% for Asset 3, we calculate the expected return and standard deviation using the following formulas:

$E(Rp)=w_1\cdot E(R_1)+w_2\cdot E(R_2)+w_3\cdot E(R_3)$

$E(Rp) = 0.3\cdot 10\%+0.3\cdot 8\%+0.4\cdot 12\%=9.8$

The portfolio variance is calculated as:

$\sigma_{p2}=w_{12}\cdot\sigma_{12}+w_{22}\cdot\sigma_{22}+w32\cdot\sigma_{32}+2\cdot w_1\cdot w_2\cdot Cov(1,2)+2\cdot w_1\cdot w_3\cdot Cov(1,3)+2\cdot w_2\cdot w_3\cdot Cov(2,3)=14.26\%$

Variable	*Value*
Expected Return	*9.8%*
Standard Deviation	*14.26%*

Example N° 26: Given Data:

Asset	*Expected Return E(R)*	*Variance (VAR)*	*Standard Deviation (σ)*
Asset 1	*12%*	$(6\%)^2$	*6%*
Asset 2	*10%*	$(4\%)^2$	*4%*

The weights for Asset 1 (aaa) and Asset 2 (1−a1 - a1−a) are provided in the following table:

Weight Distribution Table:

ρ	*P1*	*P2*	*P3*	*P4*	*P5*	*P6*
a	*0*	*20*	*40*	*60*	*80*	*100*
1−a	*100*	*80*	*60*	*40*	*20*	*0*

Task:

1. *Calculate the portfolio's expected return for different weightings as shown in the table.*
2. *Calculate the risk (variance and standard deviation) of the portfolio under the following correlation coefficient scenarios (ρ12) ρ12=−1, ρ12=−0.5, ρ12=0, ρ12=0.5, ρ12 =1*

Solution :

Expected Return of the Portfolio:

$E(Rp)= a\cdot 12\%+(1-a)\cdot 10\%$

Calculating Portfolio Variance:

$\sigma_p{}^2=a^2\cdot(6\%)^2+(1-a)^2\cdot(4\%)^2+2a(1-a)\cdot 0.6\cdot 6\%\cdot 4\%$

a (Weight in Asset 1)	*Expected Return E(Rp)*	*Correlation ρ12*	*Portfolio Variance* $\sigma_p{}^2$	*Portfolio Standard Deviation σp*
0	*10%*	*-1*	*0.0036*	*6.00%*
0.2	*10.4%*	*-0.5*	*0.0032*	*5.66%*
0.4	*10.8%*	*0*	*0.0028*	*5.29%*
0.6	*11.2%*	*0.5*	*0.0024*	*4.89%*
0.8	*11.6%*	*1*	*0.0020*	*4.47%*
1	*12%*	*1*	*0.0016*	*4.00%*

As the weight of Asset 1 increases, the expected return of the portfolio also increases. This is because Asset 1 has a higher expected return compared to Asset 2 (12% vs. 10%).

The portfolio variance and standard deviation decrease as we move towards a balanced mix between the two assets, showing the trade-off between risk and return.

The lowest risk occurs when the weight of Asset 1 is 100%, with a portfolio standard deviation of 4.00%, but this also provides the highest return of 12%.

7.2 Market model of sharpe and johnson

The market model is a statistical model introduced by william sharpe in 1943, and later enhanced by jensen in 1949. it aims to analyse the relationship between the returns of individual stocks and the market portfolio and helps measure the relationship between systematic risk (market fluctuations) and expected returns for individual assets.

- **Assumptions of the Market Model:**
  - Focus on systematic risk only: The model assumes that only systematic (market) risk affects asset returns, while unsystematic (specific) risks are not considered.
  - Linear relationship: It assumes a linear relationship between the return of a stock and the return of the market portfolio. That is, the return on the stock is influenced by the market return, based on a factor called beta (β), which represents the sensitivity of the stock's return to the market's return.
  - No mutual relationships between securities: The model assumes that returns are only related to a common factor (e.g., market returns) and not directly to other securities.
  - Market efficiency: It assumes that markets are efficient, meaning all available information is reflected in asset prices.

- Random data**:** The model assumes that returns follow random processes influenced by key market factors.

- **Model explanation**

The model is expressed as a linear relationship between the return of the stock (R_j) and the return of the market (R_m), using beta (β) to measure the relationship between the stock and the market. The basic equation of the model is:

$$R_{tj} = \alpha_j + \beta_j R_{Mt} + \varepsilon_{jt} \qquad \forall j = 1, \dots, n \qquad (29)$$

Where

- R_{tj}:Rate of return on stock j in period $\{t, t-1\}$ where j=1,2,...,n
- α_j: The unexplained return from the market (value of the rate of return on stock j when the market return is zero).
- β_j :Beta of the stock, which measures the relationship between the stock and market returns. If β = 1, the stock moves in line with the market. If β > 1, the stock is more volatile than the market; if β < 1, the stock is less volatile
- R_{Mt} :Return of the market portfolio.
- ε_{jt} : Random error (factors affecting the stock independently of the market).

Criticisms of the Sharpe-Jensen Market Model

- Assumption of market efficiency: the model assumes that markets are efficient, meaning all information is readily available to all market participants at all times. In reality, markets are often inefficient due to behavioural biases such as herd mentality or time bias.
- Over-simplified linear model: the model relies on a linear relationship between stock returns and market returns. in practice, the relationship may be non-linear

due to the complex interactions between assets and other economic factors.

- Assumption of no relationships between securities: the model assumes that asset returns are only related through their connection to the market. however, in reality, there may be relationships between stocks, such as sectoral effects or other intrinsic connections that affect returns.
- Reliance on beta as the sole measure of risk: beta is used as the sole measure of market risk, but it neglects unsystematic risks (such as company-specific risks), which can significantly influence returns.
- Random data assumption: the model assumes that returns follow random processes. in reality, returns can be influenced by unexpected or unpredictable economic factors, such as changes in government policies or financial crises.
- Excessive simplification of risk: the model simplifies risk by using beta alone, which does not fully capture the multiple types of risks that a stock may be exposed to in reality, such as liquidity risk or systemic risk.

The market model assists in measuring the relationship between asset returns and market returns using beta, and it is considered the foundation for understanding the Capital Asset Pricing Model (CAPM) and the Security Market Line (SML)

Example N° 27: You are provided with the following data for three stocks and the market portfolio. Use the Sharpe-Jensen market model to calculate the expected returns of the stocks and determine the relationship between the returns of the stocks and the market portfolio.

Stock	*Market Return (Rm) (%)*	*Stock Return (Rj) (%)*	*Beta (β)*	*Alpha (α) (%)*

A	*10%*	*12%*	*1.2*	*1.5%*
B	*10%*	*8%*	*0.8*	*2.0%*
C	*10%*	*15%*	*1.5*	*-1.0%*

Solution :The equation for the Sharpe-Jensen market model is: $R_{tj}=\alpha_j+\beta j R_{Mt}+\varepsilon_{jt}$

Calculate the Expected Return of the Stock Using the Formula:

For Stock A: $R_{tA}=\alpha_A+\beta_A \cdot R_M =1.5\%+1.2\cdot 10\%=13.5\%$

For Stock B: $R_{tB}=\alpha_B+\beta_B \cdot R_M=2.0\%+0.8\cdot 10\%=10.0\%$

For Stock C: $R_{tC}=\alpha_C+\beta_C \cdot R_M=-1.0\%+1.5\cdot 10\%=14.0\%$

Stock	*Market Return (Rm) (%)*	*Beta (β)*	*Alpha (α) (%)*	*Expected Return (Rj) (%)*
A	*10%*	*1.2*	*1.5%*	*13.5%*
B	*10%*	*0.8*	*2.0%*	*10.0%*
C	*10%*	*1.5*	*-1.0%*	*14.0%*

Stock A: Expected return of 13.5%. Since the beta is greater than 1, Stock A is more volatile than the market, and the expected return is higher.

Stock B: Expected return of 10%. The beta of 0.8 suggests that Stock B is less volatile than the market, resulting in a lower expected return.

Stock C: Expected return of 14%. With a beta of 1.5, Stock C is more volatile than the market, and the alpha is negative, indicating some unexplained factors affecting the return.

7.3 Capital Asset Pricing Model (CAPM)

This model was developed in the 1960s by Sharpe (W. Sharpe) in 1964, Treynor (J. Treynor) in 1965, Lintner (J. Lintner) in 1965, and Mossin (I. Mossin) in 1966, who developed the cognitive approach to the financial market.

- **Assumptions of the Model**

The capital asset pricing model is based on a set of simplifying assumptions that establish the theoretical framework for the model. These assumptions include:

- Systematic risk focus: the model considers only systematic risk (market risk) as relevant for pricing assets. unsystematic risk is assumed to be fully diversified away in an efficient portfolio.
- Homogeneous expectations: all investors are assumed to have the same expectations regarding the returns, variances, and covariances of all assets, implying identical assessments of risk and return.
- Perfect capital markets: financial markets are assumed to be frictionless—there are no transaction costs, taxes, or restrictions on short selling. securities are perfectly divisible and tradable.
- Risk-free borrowing and lending: investors can borrow or lend unlimited amounts at a single risk-free rate of interest, which is the same for all market participants.
- Rational and mean-variance optimising investors: investors are rational and risk-averse, and they make investment decisions solely based on the expected return and variance of portfolio returns, consistent with the mean-variance optimisation framework.
- Unlimited market access and price-taking behaviour: all investors are price takers, meaning they cannot individually influence asset prices. They can trade any quantity of assets without affecting market conditions.
- Complete information and instantaneous trading: all investors have free and simultaneous access to all relevant information, allowing them to make informed decisions. Furthermore, all assets are assumed to be perfectly liquid and can be converted into cash instantly.

These assumptions collectively establish the theoretical environment in which the CAPM operates. By focusing exclusively on systematic risk, the model simplifies the complex dynamics of financial markets, allowing for a linear relationship between expected return and market risk, as represented by beta. The assumption of homogeneous expectations ensures a unified perception of risk and return, which leads all investors to hold a combination of the market portfolio and the risk-free asset. Perfect capital markets and the availability of risk-free borrowing and lending eliminate distortions in asset pricing, enabling the derivation of the Security Market Line (SML) as a tool for evaluating the relative performance of securities. Furthermore, the presumption of rational, mean-variance optimising investors supports the notion that market prices reflect an efficient allocation of resources. While these assumptions may not fully reflect real-world conditions, they provide a foundational framework for understanding investor behaviour, portfolio construction, and equilibrium pricing in modern financial theory.

- **Portfolio Theory and the Foundation of Capital Asset Pricing Model (CAPM)**

Figure N°4: Capital Asset Pricing Model (CAPM)

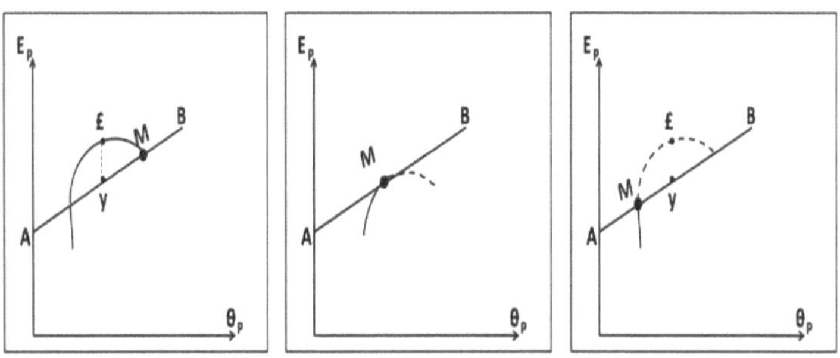

Let w_i and w_m denote the weights assigned to asset *i* and the market portfolio *m*, respectively, such that the portfolio *y* is a linear combination of the two, satisfying the condition $w_i+w_m=1$. The expected return and variance of this two-asset portfolio can be expressed as follows:

$$\begin{cases} E_{(y)}: w_i E_I + w_m . E_m \\ \sigma^2(y): w_i^2 . \sigma_i^2 + w_m^2 . \delta\sigma_m^2 + 2 w_i w_m Cov(i,m)\sigma_i\sigma_m \\ w_i + w_m = 1 \end{cases} \quad (30)$$

Where:

- *E(y):* Expected return of portfolio *y*.
- *Cov(i,m)*: The covariance between asset *i* and portfolio *M*.
- σ_m: The standard deviation of the return of portfolio *M*.
- E_I: The expected return of asset *i*.
- E_m: The expected return of portfolio *M*.

This formulation derives from Markowitz's mean-variance portfolio theory, which serves as a precursor to the Capital Asset Pricing Model (CAPM). In the context of CAPM, investors aim to optimise their portfolios by achieving the maximum expected return for a given level of risk, typically along the efficient frontier. The market portfolio MMM represents the tangency point between the efficient frontier and the Capital Market Line (CML), which includes the risk-free asset.

To quantify the sensitivity of an individual asset's return to market movements, CAPM introduces the beta coefficient, defined as:

$$\beta_i = \frac{Cov(R_i, R_m)}{Var(R_m)} \quad (31)$$

Where:

- B_i Beta of asset *i*.
- R_i, R_m : Returns of asset *i* and the market.

- $Cov(R_i,R_m)$: Covariance between asset *i*'s return and the market return.
- $Var(R_m)$: Variance of the market return.

Demonstrates that beta measures the sensitivity of an asset's return relative to the return of the market. It is crucial to note that beta quantifies how much the return on asset R_i moves in relation to the market's return R_m . If $\beta>1$, the asset is more volatile than the market; if $\beta<1$, the asset is less volatile than the market. A β value of 1 indicates that the asset moves in line with the market.

The Capital Asset Pricing Model (CAPM) reflects the relationship between return and risk using the beta coefficient as a measure of risk. The CAPM is then formulated by the following equation:

$$R_i = R_F + \beta\left(R_m - R_F\right) \tag{32}$$

Where:

- R_i: The rate of return of the stock.
- R_F: The risk-free rate of return.
- β: The beta of the stock, which measures the sensitivity of the stock's return to the market return.
- R_m: The market rate of return, which is the average rate of return of stock prices in the market.

A part of this equation, $(R_m - R_F)\beta$, links the risk premium (R_{pm}) to beta (β), which represents the degree of risk. As beta increases, the risk premium also increases, and therefore, higher returns are expected in exchange for accepting increased risk.

CAPM plays a fundamental role in asset pricing and portfolio management by establishing a direct linear relationship between risk and return under equilibrium conditions. It allows investors and analysts to assess whether a security is fairly valued relative to its risk exposure.

- **Criticisms of the Capital Asset Pricing Model (CAPM)**

Despite its theoretical elegance and foundational role in modern finance, the CAPM has been subject to extensive empirical and conceptual criticism. One of the primary concerns relates to its over-simplified assumptions, particularly the reliance on a single risk factor—systematic market risk—while neglecting other influential factors such as firm size, value characteristics, and momentum, which have been found to explain asset returns more effectively, as highlighted by the Fama-French multi-factor models.

Additionally, CAPM assumes homogeneous expectations and rational investor behaviour, which fail to capture the complexities of real-world decision-making. Behavioural finance literature has demonstrated that investors are often influenced by cognitive biases such as overconfidence, loss aversion, and herd behaviour, none of which are accommodated by the model.

The model's dependence on historical beta estimates also raises concerns. Since beta is not stable over time and may change with market conditions or company-specific developments, its predictive reliability is questionable. Furthermore, the assumption of a risk-free asset, which investors can borrow or lend at a fixed rate, is unrealistic, especially in markets subject to inflation, credit risk, and interest rate volatility.

Another point of criticism is the model's static nature, which assumes constant risk-return relationships over time. In practice, financial markets are dynamic and influenced by evolving macroeconomic and geopolitical factors. Moreover, CAPM's presumption of perfect capital markets—with no taxes, transaction costs, or information asymmetries—rarely holds true in real investment environments.

Lastly, empirical studies have consistently shown that the security market line (SML) predicted by CAPM does not always align with observed returns, especially for small-cap or distressed stocks, calling into question the model's descriptive and predictive validity.

Example N° 28: Assume the risk-free rate (R_f) is 5%, and the market return (R_m) is 12%. The betas for the stocks are provided, and you are asked to compute the expected returns using the CAPM equation.

Asset	*Beta (β)*	*Expected Return of the Market (Rm) (%)*	*Risk-Free Rate (Rf) (%)*
A	*1.2*	*12%*	*5%*
B	*0.8*	*12%*	*5%*
C	*1.5*	*12%*	*5%*

Solution : Expected Return (CAPM) (%)

For Asset A: $R_A = 5\% + 1.2 \cdot (12\% - 5\%) = 13.4\ \%$

For Asset B: $R_B = 5\% + 0.8 \cdot (12\% - 5\%) = 10.6\%$

For Asset C: $R_C = 5\% + 1.5 \cdot (12\% - 5\%) = 15.5\%$

- *Asset A has a beta of 1.2, indicating it is more volatile than the market. According to the CAPM, the expected return of Asset A is 13.4%, reflecting its higher risk.*
- *Asset B has a beta of 0.8, meaning it is less volatile than the market. The expected return for Asset B is 10.6%, reflecting its lower risk.*
- *Asset C, with a beta of 1.5, is more volatile than the market, and as such, its expected return is 15.5%, reflecting its higher level of risk.*

7.5 Security Market Line (SML)

The SML is a graphical representation in the Capital Asset Pricing Model (CAPM), showing the relationship between the expected return of assets and systematic risk (measured by beta).

The SML illustrates the linear relationship between expected returns and beta (i.e., systematic risk), indicating that the return on a stock depends on its beta, which reflects the stock's sensitivity to market risk.

The slope of the Security Market Line (SML) represents the investor's degree of Risk Aversion. The steeper the SML, the greater the investor's tendency to avoid risk. Conversely, when the SML is flatter (i.e., has a smaller slope), the investor's risk aversion is lower.

If the portfolio consists solely of risk-free assets, the return will be equal to the risk-free return (RF). However, if the portfolio contains risky assets, the investor expects to earn an additional return called the Risk Premium. s shown in the following figure:

Figure N°5: Risk Premium

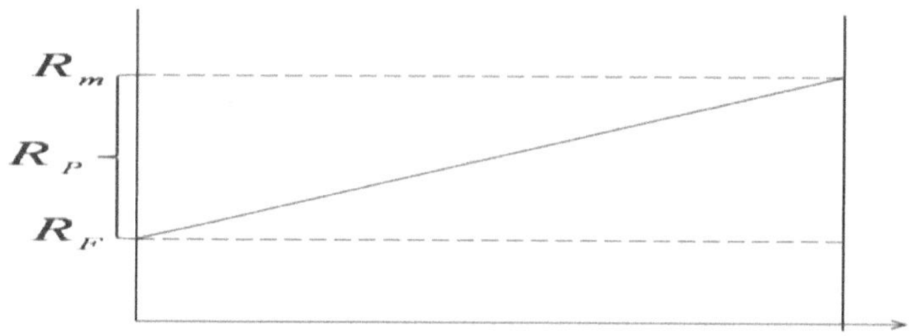

- R_P: Risk Premium
- R_m: Rate of return on the market portfolio measured by a market index
- R_F: Rate of return on a risk-free asset, such as treasury bills or government bonds.

The risk premium is achieved by taking on the risk of the portfolio, and the best return for the risk is the standard deviation of the available instruments in the market. It can be calculated by the following formula:

If the risk of the market portfolio is denoted as σ, the slope of the CML is calculated by the following equation:

$$R_p = R_m - R_F \quad (33)$$

Example N° 29: You are an investor looking to determine the expected return on investments in three assets using the Security Market Line (SML). You are given the following data:

Asset	Beta (β)	Expected Market Return (Rm) (%)	Risk-Free Rate (RF) (%)
A	1.2	10%	4%
B	0.8	10%	4%
C	1.5	10%	4%

Tasks:

1. *Calculate the expected return for each asset using the SML equation.*
2. *Calculate the Risk Premium for each asset.*
3. *Draw the Security Market Line (SML) using these assets.*

Solution:

Use the SML Equation to Calculate the Expected Return for Each Asset

- For Asset A: $R_A=4\%+1.2\cdot(10\%-4\%)=11.2\%$
- For Asset B: $R_B=4\%+0.8\cdot(10\%-4\%)=8.8\%$
- For Asset C: $R_C=4\%+1.5\cdot(10\%-4\%)=13\%$

Calculate the Risk Premium for Each Asset

Risk Premium= $=R_m-R_f=10\%-4\%=6\%$

Plot the Security Market Line (SML)

Asset	*Beta (β)*	*Expected Return (SML) (%)*	*Risk Premium (%)*
A	*1.2*	*11.2%*	*6%*
B	*0.8*	*8.8%*	*6%*
C	*1.5*	*13.0%*	*6%*

1. Asset A has a beta of 1.2, indicating it is more volatile than the market, and its expected return is 11.2%.
2. Asset B has a beta of 0.8, indicating it is less volatile than the market, and its expected return is 8.8%.

3. Asset C has a beta of 1.5, indicating it is more volatile than the market, and its expected return is 13.0%.

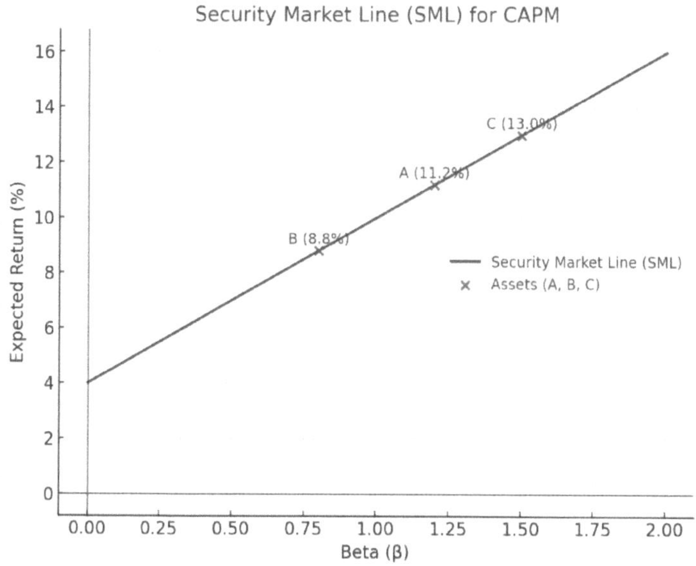

Here is the Security Market Line (SML), showing the relationship between beta (β) and expected return. The red points represent the three assets (A, B, and C) with their corresponding beta and expected return. The blue line is the SML, illustrating the linear relationship between risk (beta) and expected return as per the CAPM.

7.5 Capital Market Line (CML) Model

- **Assumptions of the Capital Market Line (CML) Model:**
  - Risk-free asset: The model assumes the existence of a risk-free asset, which offers a fixed return with zero risk. This asset is assumed to be available for borrowing or lending in unlimited quantities at the risk-free rate.

- Efficient market: The model assumes that all investors have access to the same information and that financial markets are efficient, meaning that asset prices reflect all available information.
- Investors are rational: investors are assumed to be rational and risk-averse. they aim to maximise the expected return for a given level of risk or minimise risk for a given level of return.
- Perfect substitution between risk-free asset and risky portfolio: the model assumes that investors can freely combine a risk-free asset with a portfolio of risky assets to form an optimal portfolio, known as the market portfolio.
- Homogeneous expectations: it is assumed that all investors have the same expectations regarding the return, risk, and correlation of assets.
- No transaction costs: the model assumes that there are no transaction costs (such as brokerage fees or taxes) in buying and selling assets.
- Single-period investment horizon: the model assumes a single investment period, meaning that the time horizon for investment decisions is fixed.
- No arbitrage opportunities: there are no arbitrage opportunities, meaning there are no ways to earn riskless profit without any capital investment.

• **The Relationship Between Risk and Return in the Capital Market Line (CML)**

  - **Capital Market Line (CML)**

To choose the optimal portfolio, investors select a portfolio on the Capital Market Line (CML), where the expected return of the portfolio is related to the risk it bears (measured by standard deviation), considering a portfolio that includes both risk-free assets and risky assets.

Figure N°6: Capital Market Line (CML)

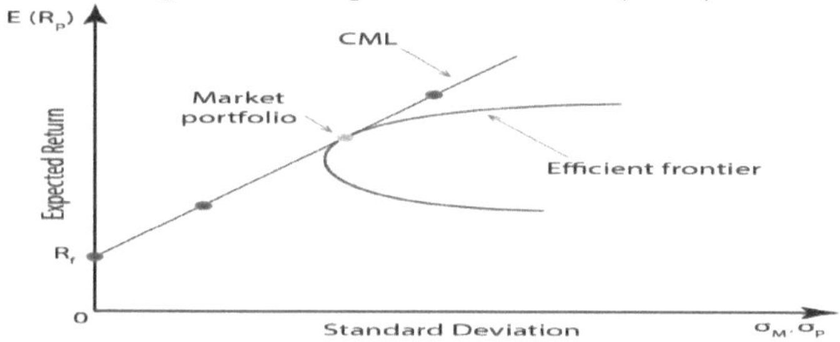

This line represents the Capital Market Line (CML), and each point on it represents a portfolio. The CML allows us to depict the set of efficient portfolios that combine risk-free assets with risky financial assets. Point M represents the point of tangency with the capital market line and is referred to as the Efficient Portfolio Curve.

If the risk is for the market portfolio, then the slope of the CML is calculated using the following equation:

$$slop\ CML = \frac{R_m - R_F}{\delta_m} \tag{34}$$

Figure N°7: Impact of the Slope of the Capital Market Line on Portfolio Return

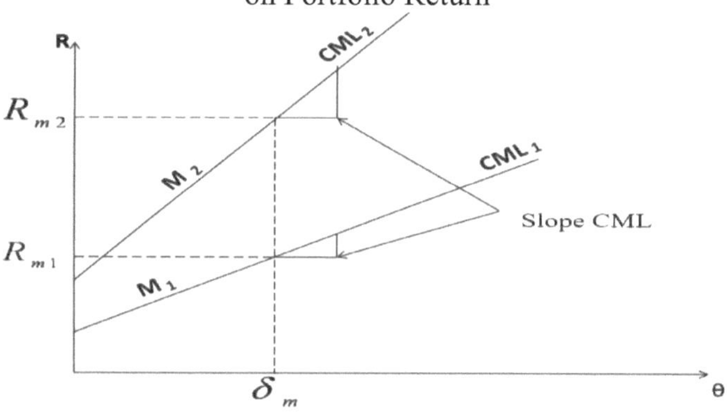

As shown in Figure 7, as the slope of the Capital Market Line increases, the return rises from R_{m1} to R_{m2}, assuming that the portfolio's risk remains constant.

Figure N°8: Capital Market Line

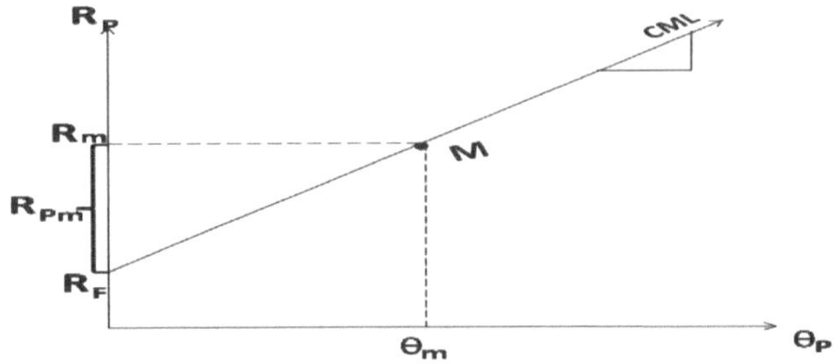

Thus, the Capital Market Line demonstrates the balanced relationship between the returns of the efficient portfolio and the risks associated with it, as shown in Figure 8. The Capital Market Line extends as a straight line from the risk-free return (RF) to the optimal portfolio at point M. At equilibrium, the expected return of the financial portfolio will be equal to the result of the following equation:

$$R_p = R_F + \delta_P \frac{R_m - R_F}{\delta_m} \qquad (35)$$

Where:

- R_p: Expected return of the financial portfolio
- R_m: Expected return of the market portfolio
- δ_m: Standard deviation of portfolio returns
- R_F: Risk-free return

- **Criticisms of the Capital Market Line (CML) Model**

while the Capital Market Line model offers a foundational framework for understanding the risk-return trade-off in portfolio management, it faces significant criticisms due to its assumptions and simplifications:

- Real-world infeasibility of risk-free assets: The assumption of a risk-free asset with a constant return is unrealistic in practice. No financial asset is truly risk-free, and government bonds, typically considered risk-free, still carry some risk, including interest rate risk and inflation risk.
- Assumption of rationality: The assumption that all investors are perfectly rational is widely criticised. In reality, investors may exhibit irrational behaviour due to biases such as overconfidence, loss aversion, or herd mentality, which contradicts the assumptions of the CML model.
- Homogeneous expectations: The assumption that all investors have identical expectations about the future returns and risks of assets is unrealistic. Investors may have different information, risk preferences, and interpretations of market conditions.
- No transaction costs: The assumption that there are no transaction costs is overly simplistic. In real-world markets, transaction costs, including taxes, fees, and bid-ask spreads, can significantly impact portfolio returns, especially for frequent traders.
- Single-period investment horizon: The model assumes a single-period investment horizon, which is limiting. In reality, investors typically have multi-period investment horizons, and the risk-return trade-off may differ over time.
- Market efficiency: The CML assumes perfect market efficiency, meaning all information is reflected in asset prices. However, real markets are often characterised by inefficiencies due to factors such as behavioural biases, insider information, and market manipulation.
- Over-simplification of risk: The model simplifies the risk by considering it only in terms of standard

deviation, but this does not capture all types of risk, such as liquidity risk, market risk, or systemic risk. This oversimplification may lead to poor investment decisions in complex, real-world scenarios.

- Exclusion of other asset classes: The model assumes only risky assets and a risk-free asset, ignoring the possibility of other asset classes, such as real estate or commodities, which may offer diversification benefits.
- Excessive dependence on historical data: The CML relies heavily on past data to predict future returns and risks, which may not be reliable. Past performance is not always indicative of future results, and the model may fail to adapt to sudden market changes.

Example N° 30: You are an investor looking to construct an optimal portfolio by selecting a combination of a risk-free asset and a market portfolio. You are given the following data:

- *Risk-free rate (RF): 4%*
- *Expected market return (Rm): 10%*
- *Standard deviation of market portfolio (δm): 15%*
- *Standard deviation of the risky portfolio (δp): 20%*

Tasks:

1. *Calculate the slope of the Capital Market Line (CML)*
2. *Using the slope, calculate the expected return of the financial portfolio R_p that combines the market portfolio with the risk-free asset for a given level of risk.*
3. *Plot the Capital Market Line (CML) to visualise the relationship between the expected return and risk for various combinations of the risk-free asset and the market portfolio.*

Solution:

Calculate the Slope of the CML

Given: R_m*=10,* R_F*=4%, δm=15%*
We substitute these values into the formula:
slope of CML=10%−4%15%=0.4
Calculate the Expected Return of the Portfolio (Rp)
The expected return of the financial portfolio Rp with risk levels (standard deviations) of 0%, 10%, 15%, 20%, and 25%.

1. *For* δ_p*=0% (Risk-free asset): Rp=4%+0.4×0=4%*
2. *For* δ_p*=10%: Rp=4%+0.4×10%=8%*
3. *For* δ_p*=15%:* R_p*=4%+0.4×15%=10%*
4. *For δp=20%: Rp=4%+0.4×20%=12%*
5. *For δp=25%: Rp=4%+0.4×25%=14%*

Plot the Capital Market Line (CML):

Portfolio Risk (δp) (%)	*Expected Return (Rp) (%)*
0%	*4%*
10%	*8%*
15%	*10%*
20%	*12%*
25%	*14%*

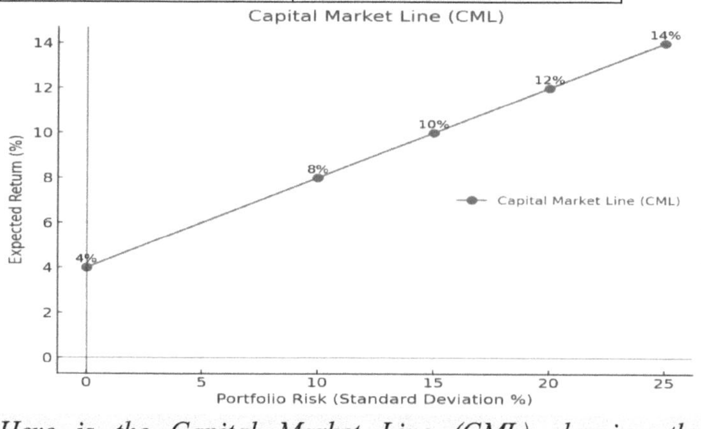

Here is the Capital Market Line (CML) showing the relationship between portfolio risk (standard deviation) and expected return. As the portfolio's risk increases, the expected

return also increases, following the linear relationship depicted by the CML. The slope of the line represents the trade-off between risk and return in an efficient market.

7.6 The Fama-French 3 Factor Model

The Fama-French 3 Factor Model is a well-established asset pricing model that extends the Capital Asset Pricing Model (CAPM) by incorporating additional risk factors. It aims to provide a more comprehensive explanation of stock returns by considering factors beyond market risk alone.

- **Estimation Form of the Model**

  The three factors in the Fama-French model are:
  - RPM (Risk Premium): The difference between the returns on a diversified market portfolio (value-weighted CRSP returns) and a risk-free return. This factor captures the market risk premium.
  - SMB (Small Minus Big): The difference in returns between diversified portfolios of small-cap and large-cap stocks. This factor accounts for the size effect, where smaller firms tend to offer higher returns than larger firms.
  - HML (High Minus Low): The difference in returns between diversified portfolios of high book-to-market (B/M) stocks (often considered value stocks) and low B/M stocks (growth stocks). This factor reflects the value effect, where stocks with higher book-to-market ratios tend to outperform those with lower ratios.

  The model in its estimation form is:

$$R_{i,t} - R_{f,t} = \alpha_i + \beta_{i,m}(RPM_T) + \beta_{i,sml}(SML_T) + \beta_{i,hml}(HML_T) + \varepsilon_{i,t} \qquad (36)$$

Where:

- $R_{i,t}$:represents the utility stock return during period ttt.

- $R_{f,t}$,: is the return on the risk-free asset.
- α_i :is the intercept term, which should theoretically be zero.
- βi: for each factor.
  - $\beta_{i,m}$: corresponds to the CAPM beta, which measures the relationship between the asset's return and the market return.
  - $\beta_{i,sml}$ and $\beta_{i,hml}$ represent the Small Minus Big (SMB) and High Minus Low (HML) factors, respectively.
- $\varepsilon_{i,t}$ the regression error term.

- **Criticisms of the Fama-French 3 Factor Model**

Despite its contribution to asset pricing theory, the Fama-French 3 Factor Model has faced several criticisms based on empirical studies and practical limitations:

- Limited General Applicability: The model performs well for US-based equity markets, but its applicability to international markets remains questionable. Studies have shown that the factors driving returns in the US may not have the same impact in emerging or developed markets (e.g., Europe or Asia). This discrepancy has led researchers to argue that the model may not adequately account for country-specific risks and market inefficiencies. For example, a study by Aspris et al. (2015) highlighted that the value premium (HML) and size premium (SMB) factors do not exhibit the same predictive power in European markets as they do in the US.
- Inconsistent Factor Performance: While the model explains a significant portion of cross-sectional returns, the factors—size (SMB) and value (HML)—do not consistently perform well in all periods. Specifically, the size effect (small-cap stocks outperforming large-cap stocks) has diminished in recent decades. In particular, small-cap stocks have underperformed

large-cap stocks since the late 1990s, leading to scepticism about the robustness of the SMB factor. A study by Fama and French (2015) themselves acknowledged that the size and value premiums have significantly weakened over the last two decades, raising questions about the long-term stability of the model's key factors.

- Exclusion of Other Risk Factors: Although the Fama-French 3 Factor Model is an improvement on CAPM, it still fails to incorporate all potential risk factors that could influence stock returns. Factors such as momentum, liquidity, and macroeconomic variables (e.g., interest rates, inflation) have been shown to have explanatory power for returns that the model does not capture. The Carhart Four-Factor Model (1997) addresses this issue by adding a momentum factor. Studies, such as those by Stambaugh and Yu (2019), have shown that momentum is an important predictor of stock returns that the Fama-French model overlooks.
- Estimation Issues: The accuracy of factor betas (β\betaβ) estimates, which are central to the model, depends heavily on the quality and frequency of the underlying data. When using data over short periods or in volatile market conditions, factor betas can exhibit instability, reducing the model's effectiveness in predicting future returns. Additionally, R-squared values for the 3-factor model are often low (as evidenced by the data in earlier discussions). A low R-squared suggests that the model does not fully explain the variation in stock returns, and there may be misspecification or missing variables.
- The Model's Static Nature: The Fama-French model assumes that the relationship between factors and stock returns is constant over time, but financial markets are

dynamic and subject to changes in economic conditions, investor behaviour, and market structure. As pointed out by Berk and DeMarzo (2017), the model's static framework does not account for changes in investor preferences or the changing nature of risk premiums over time.

- Factor timing: the ability to adjust exposure to factors based on macroeconomic conditions—has been suggested as a necessary addition to make the model more realistic in today's rapidly evolving markets.
- Data Issues and Over fitting: The model has been criticised for being overfitted to historical data. When parameters are estimated based on historical data, there is always the risk of fitting a model too closely to past patterns, leading to poor out-of-sample forecasting performance. The data mining criticism is often raised, as many models—Fama-French included—tend to find patterns that may be specific to a certain period, but are not predictive of future returns.
- Challenges in Utility Ratemaking: Although the model is increasingly used in utility ratemaking, where it helps estimate the cost of equity, the assumptions of efficient markets and perfect competition rarely hold in regulated industries. Factors like market power and regulatory risk can significantly impact utility firms' returns, which are not captured by the Fama-French factors.

Example N°31: You are an analyst tasked with using the Fama-French 3 Factor Model to estimate the expected return of a stock. You are provided with the following data for a particular stock over a certain period:

Stock	*Return (Ri,t) (%)*	*Risk-Free Rate (Rf,t) (%)*	*RPM (Risk Premium) (%)*	*SMB (Small Minus Big) (%)*	*HML (High Minus Low) (%)*
A	*12%*	*3%*	*5%*	*2%*	*4%*
B	*10%*	*3%*	*5%*	*1%*	*3%*
C	*15%*	*3%*	*5%*	*3%*	*5%*

Tasks:

1. *Estimate the Expected Return for each stock using the Fama-French 3 Factor Model. Assume the following factor betas for each stock:*
   - *Stock A:* $\beta_{A,m}=1.2$, $\beta_{A,sml}=0.5\beta A,hml=0.7$
   - *Stock B:* $\beta_{B,m}=1.0$, $\beta_{B,sml}=0.3$, $\beta_{B,hml}=0.4$
   - *Stock C:* $\beta_{C,m}=1.3$, $\beta_{C,sml}=0.4$, $\beta_{C,hml}=0.6$
2. *Interpret the results of the expected returns for each stock based on their factor loadings.*

Solution:

Apply the Fama-French 3 Factor Model For each stock, the expected return :

For Stock A: $R_{A,t}-R_{f,t}=0+(1.2\cdot5\%)+(0.5\cdot2\%)+(0.7\cdot4\%)=12.8\%$

For Stock B: $R_{B,t}-R_{f,t}=0+(1.0\cdot5\%)+(0.3\cdot1\%)+(0.4\cdot3\%)=9.5\%$

For Stock C: $R_{C,t}-R_{f,t}=0+(1.3\cdot5\%)+(0.4\cdot3\%)+(0.6\cdot5\%)=13.7\%$

Stock	*Risk-Free Rate (Rf,t) (%)*	*RPM (Risk Premium) (%)*	*SMB (Small Minus Big) (%)*	*HML (High Minus Low) (%)*	*Expected Return (Ri,t) (%)*
A	*3%*	*5%*	*2%*	*4%*	*12.8%*
B	*3%*	*5%*	*1%*	*3%*	*9.5%*
C	*3%*	*5%*	*3%*	*5%*	*13.7%*

- *Stock A has the highest expected return at 12.8%, driven by its relatively high market risk beta (1.2) and value factor (HML = 0.7).*
- *Stock B has a more moderate expected return of 9.5%, influenced by lower market risk (beta of 1.0) and lower values for the size and value factors.*
- *Stock C has the highest return of 13.7%, due to its higher market risk beta (1.3) and moderately high size and value factors.*

7.7 Arbitrage Pricing Theory (APT) Model

The Arbitrage Pricing Theory (APT), introduced by Ross in 1976, is an alternative to the Capital Asset Pricing Model (CAPM). More specifically, it is considered a special case of the broader arbitrage pricing theory.

- **Assumptions of the APT Model:**

The concept of "arbitrage" in this model implies that each factor affects the rate of return on a security. However, this does not mean that the model does not rely on specific assumptions. It assumes the following:

- Perfect competition in the capital market: The model assumes that all traded securities are in a market characterised by perfect competition.
- Multiple participants' influence: A large number of investors and traders play a significant role in influencing security prices, with the goal of increasing wealth under conditions of certainty.
- Investor preference for wealth maximisation: Investors aim to maximise wealth under conditions of certainty.
- Linear relationship of returns: The return on a security can be expressed as a linear function of a set of key factors or economic indicators.

- **The General Framework of the APT Model:**

The APT model introduces the influence of both external economic factors and internal company-specific factors on the rate of return of securities. It assumes that these factors have varying degrees of impact on the expected return of securities, depending on the nature of each security and its sensitivity to these factors.

The model uses risk factors, which are the primary economic influences on security prices. These risk factors can be general economic factors (such as inflation, interest rate changes), or company-specific factors (such as leverage, operational efficiency, or management quality). Each of these factors has an impact on the return of the security.

The following equation is used to model the returns in the APT framework:

$$R = E + bF + \varepsilon \tag{37}$$

Where:

- R: Actual return on the security.
- E: Expected return on the security.
- b: Sensitivity of the security to changes in the risk factors.
- F: Risk factors influencing the security.
- ε: The residual or unsystematic risk (error term).

This equation assumes that the actual return of a security is equal to the expected return plus the sensitivity to the changing factors, along with the residual risk.

- Factors Influencing the Model: If there are three or four factors that affect the adequacy of the model, and influence the market returns, the model would appear as:

$$R = E(R) + \beta_1 F_1 + \beta_2 F_2 + \cdots . \beta_k F_k + \varepsilon \tag{38}$$

Where:

- $\beta_1, \beta_2, \ldots \beta_k$: Sensitivities to various factors.
- $F_1, F_2, \ldots F_k$:Risk factors affecting the security.

- **Criticisms of the APT Model:**

While the APT model offers a more comprehensive approach compared to the CAPM, it has faced criticisms for several reasons:

- Limited General Applicability: The model works well in the US equity markets, but its applicability to international markets is questionable. Studies have shown that the factors driving returns in the US may not have the same impact in emerging or developed markets (e.g., Europe or Asia). This discrepancy raises concerns about the model's effectiveness in capturing country-specific risks and market inefficiencies.
- Inconsistent Factor Performance: While the model explains a significant portion of cross-sectional returns, the size (SMB) and value (HML) factors do not always perform consistently over time. In recent decades, the size effect (where small-cap stocks outperform large-cap stocks) has weakened, leading to scepticism about the robustness of the SMB factor. Studies by Fama and French (2015) themselves noted the diminishing size and value premiums in recent years, questioning the long-term stability of these factors.
- Exclusion of Other Risk Factors: The APT model, although an improvement over CAPM, still excludes other potential risk factors, such as momentum, liquidity, and macroeconomic variables (e.g., inflation or interest rates). The Carhart Four-Factor Model (1997) addresses this by adding a momentum factor, showing that momentum can significantly influence stock returns, which APT overlooks.
- Estimation Issues: The accuracy of the beta coefficients (β\betaβ) in the model heavily depends on the quality and frequency of the data. When using data over short periods or in volatile market conditions, the factor betas

can show instability, reducing the model's effectiveness in predicting future returns. Additionally, low R-squared values often suggest that the model fails to fully explain variations in stock returns, potentially due to omitted variables.

- Static Nature of the Model: The APT model assumes a constant relationship between the factors and stock returns. However, financial markets are dynamic, and the risk-return relationship can change over time due to evolving economic conditions, market structure, and investor preferences. The model does not account for such changes, which limits its real-world applicability.
- Data Issues and Overfitting: The model has been criticised for overfitting to historical data, leading to potential problems with out-of-sample forecasting. The model may find patterns that are specific to a certain period but do not predict future returns accurately.
- Challenges in Application to Regulated Industries: Although the APT model is increasingly used in utility ratemaking, the assumptions of efficient markets and perfect competition do not always hold in regulated industries. In such markets, factors like market power and regulatory risk can significantly affect returns, but these are not captured by the APT model.

While the APT model provides a more nuanced approach to asset pricing by incorporating multiple risk factors beyond market risk, it is not without its limitations. The exclusion of important factors, along with challenges related to its application in different markets, highlight the need for further refinement and the inclusion of additional risk factors for more accurate pricing of financial assets.

Chapter Eight
Portfolio Performance Evaluation

Chapter Eight: Portfolio Performance Evaluation

Portfolio decisions are determined based on its objectives, and when making a decision, either the purchase or sale of available instruments is carried out. This is done to assess and evaluate the results of the decisions made, ensuring the accuracy or error of these decisions and their impact on achieving the objectives.

8.1 Principles of Financial Portfolio Evaluation

The evaluation process is governed by a set of fundamental principles, the most important of which are as follows:

- Comparing actual performance with expected performance, which is done by relying on financial market mechanisms, considering the sensitivity of the instruments within the portfolio to market risks.
- Measuring the value of the portfolio assets based on their market value or intrinsic value of the instruments, rather than their original cost.
- Taking into account distributed profits and expected future distributions, in addition to total returns, actual realized and unrealized capital and income gains and losses, which arise due to market value fluctuations of the investment instruments.
- Comparing the portfolio's performance with the financial market's performance, whether the index is domestic or external. Portfolio evaluation, when compared with the market line, indicates whether performance is good. If the portfolio's performance is higher than the market line, the performance is good; if the return is on the market line, the performance is acceptable; if the portfolio's return is below the market line, the performance is not acceptable.

- **8.2 Sharpe Model (1966)**

William Sharpe introduced a composite measure for evaluating the performance of securities portfolios based on return and risk. This measure, known as the Reward-to-Variability ratio, assesses portfolio performance by comparing the reward (return) to the risk (variability). If the expected return is insufficient, the investor may choose an alternative investment or opt for a risk-free investment with the same return as the risky one.

Therefore, Sharpe evaluates portfolio performance by compensating one unit of risk with the excess return over that risk, and the greater the variability of return, the better the portfolio's performance.

$$S_{harp} = \frac{R_p - R_F}{\delta} \qquad (39)$$

Where:

- R_P: Portfolio return.
- R_F: Risk-free return.
- δ: Standard deviation of the portfolio's return relative to the market return.

The following figure illustrates the performance of investment portfolios compared to the performance of the market index.

Figure N°9: Graphical Measurement of Performance According to Sharpe.

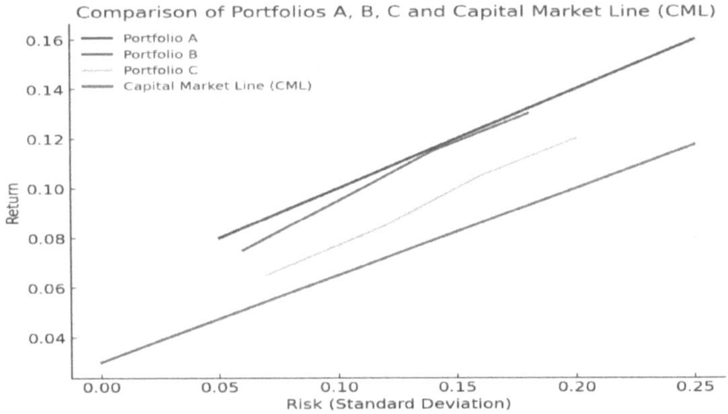

The Sharpe ratio allows for the comparison of the performance of three portfolios, A, B, and C, and compares them with the performance of the market index. From this, we observe that the portfolios perform better than the market index, with portfolio A outperforming B, and portfolio B outperforming C.

Criticisms of the Sharpe Ratio for Portfolio Performance Evaluation : The Sharpe Ratio is one of the most commonly used tools to evaluate the performance of investment portfolios based on return relative to risk. However, despite its widespread use, several criticisms have been directed towards this model. Below are some of the key criticisms:

- Assumption of Normally Distributed Returns: The Sharpe Ratio assumes that financial returns follow a normal distribution (Gaussian distribution). This assumption can be inaccurate in many financial markets where returns often exhibit greater volatility or "fat tails". This means that the model may either overestimate or underestimate risk in certain cases.
- Failure to Differentiate Between Positive and Negative Risk: The Sharpe Ratio treats all types of risk (both

positive and negative) in the same manner. In reality, some investors may be more concerned with negative risks (potential losses) rather than positive risks (opportunities for higher returns). The Sharpe Ratio does not differentiate between these two types of risk, which may lead to a less nuanced assessment.

- Reliance on Standard Deviation as a Risk Measure: The model uses standard deviation (SD) as a measure of risk, but this may not always accurately reflect the true risk faced by an investor. Risk can often be asymmetric, and some risks may be more severe than others, which the standard deviation alone does not capture.
- Exclusion of Non-Financial Factors: The Sharpe Ratio focuses primarily on financial returns and risks, but it overlooks other important factors such as liquidity, timing, and broader economic conditions that can significantly impact portfolio performance.
- Dependence on the Risk-Free Rate: The model assumes the risk-free rate as a constant, typically using government bond yields or similar risk-free instruments. However, this rate can fluctuate over time and vary across different economic environments, which can impact the accuracy of the Sharpe Ratio.
- Reliance on Expected Returns: The Sharpe Ratio is based on expected returns, which are estimates that can often be imprecise or change over time. The model can therefore be highly sensitive to changes in market conditions or new information that may affect future returns.
- Does Not Account for Correlation Between Assets: The Sharpe Ratio does not take into account the interactions between assets within a portfolio (i.e., the correlation between assets). This means the model may fail to recognise portfolios that are well-diversified or those

with different risk-return characteristics that could optimise overall risk.

Example N°32: You are given three investment portfolios with their expected returns, standard deviations (volatility), and a risk-free rate. Use the Sharpe Ratio to evaluate the performance of these portfolios.

Portfolio	*Expected Return (R_p)*	*Risk-Free Rate (R_f)*	*Standard Deviation (σ_p)*
A	*0.12 (12%)*	*0.05 (5%)*	*0.08 (8%)*
B	*0.14 (14%)*	*0.05 (5%)*	*0.10 (10%)*
C	*0.10 (10%)*	*0.05 (5%)*	*0.05 (5%)*

Solution: Calculating the Sharpe Ratio
Portfolio A: Sharpe Ratio A=(0.12−0.05)/0.08=0.875, indicating a moderate risk-adjusted return.
Portfolio B: Sharpe Ratio B=(0.14−0.05)/0.10=0.90 suggesting a slightly better risk-adjusted return than Portfolio A.
Portfolio C: Sharpe Ratio C=(0.10−0.05)/0.05=1.00, indicating the best risk-adjusted return among the three portfolios.

A higher Sharpe Ratio means a better risk-adjusted return, meaning that Portfolio C is the most efficient in terms of return per unit of risk.

8.3 Trynor's Performance Measure (1965)

The Trynor's Performance Measure, introduced by Jack Treynor in 1965, is a tool used to evaluate the performance of an investment portfolio based on the Capital Asset Pricing Model (CAPM). This model assumes that when the actual return on an investment equals its expected return, the portfolio's risk is only due to systematic (market-related) risk. In this framework, the risk of the portfolio is measured by its beta (β), where the beta of the market index is set to 1.

The Treynor Ratio is calculated using the following formula:

$$T = \frac{R_P - R_F}{\beta} \quad (40)$$

Where:

- R_p : Portfolio return
- R_f: Risk-free rate (the return on a risk-free asset)
- β_p : Beta of the portfolio, which measures the portfolio's sensitivity to the overall market movements

The Treynor Ratio is used to assess how much excess return a portfolio generates per unit of risk taken, as measured by its beta.

Higher Treynor Ratio (T): A higher ratio indicates better performance. It means the portfolio is generating more return for each unit of systematic risk (market risk) it assumes.

Lower Treynor Ratio (T): A lower ratio suggests poor performance, meaning the portfolio is not providing sufficient return for the risk it is bearing.

Key Assumptions:

- The Treynor Ratio assumes that the market is efficient, and the portfolio is only subject to systematic risk (market risk).
- It does not consider unsystematic (company-specific) risk, which is diversified away in a well-diversified portfolio.

Criticisms of the Treynor Ratio for Evaluating Portfolio Performance :The Treynor Ratio is a popular measure used to evaluate the risk-adjusted return of investment portfolios, based on systematic (market) risk. However, there are several criticisms and limitations associated with this measure:

- The Treynor Ratio only considers systematic risk (market risk) and ignores unsystematic risk (specific risk related to individual assets or companies). In reality, many portfolios have a significant amount of unsystematic risk that may not be captured by the Treynor Ratio. If a portfolio is not well-diversified, the unsystematic risk may significantly affect the portfolio's performance, and the Treynor Ratio will fail to reflect this.

- The Treynor Ratio assumes that the portfolio is sufficiently diversified to eliminate unsystematic risk. This assumption may not hold in portfolios that are concentrated in a few assets or industries. : For portfolios with limited diversification, the Treynor Ratio may not give an accurate picture of performance, as unsystematic risk may still be a significant factor.
- The Treynor Ratio tends to favour portfolios with higher betas, as it uses beta as a measure of risk. This means that portfolios with higher market risk (i.e., more volatile) may appear to perform better according to the Treynor Ratio, even though they are riskier. The Treynor Ratio might give higher values to portfolios that are more sensitive to market fluctuations, leading to a biased evaluation if the focus is only on systematic risk.
- The Treynor Ratio does not account for the absolute return of a portfolio. A portfolio might have a high Treynor Ratio but still deliver low absolute returns, which might be unacceptable to certain investors.

The ratio focuses on the return per unit of market risk, but it does not show whether the portfolio's total return is adequate. Some investors may be more concerned with absolute returns than with risk-adjusted returns.

- The Treynor Ratio is based on expected returns, which are estimates that can often be imprecise or fluctuate over time. The ratio's reliability depends on the accuracy of the expected return inputs, and changes in these expectations can lead to significant variations in the ratio, making it less stable or reliable in volatile market conditions.

- The Treynor Ratio assumes that capital markets are efficient, meaning that all available information is reflected in asset prices. This assumption might not hold in real-world markets, where information asymmetries or market inefficiencies may exist. In inefficient markets, the Treynor Ratio may not accurately capture the risk-adjusted performance, as prices may not fully reflect the available information.
- The Treynor Ratio does not account for the time dimension of risk or returns. A portfolio might perform well in the short term but have high volatility or underperform over a longer time horizon, which is not reflected in the Treynor Ratio. The ratio is more effective for short-term performance measurement, but it may not provide a full picture of how a portfolio will perform under different market conditions or over longer periods.

Example N°33: The following table shows the expected return ,beta, and the risk-free rate for five different portfolios (A, B, C, D, and E). The market return is also provided.

Portfolio	*Expected Return* $E(R_p)$	*Beta* β_p	*Risk-Free Rate* R_f	*Market Return* R_m
A	*10%*	*1.2*	*3%*	*8%*
B	*12%*	*0.9*	*3%*	*8%*
C	*14%*	*1.5*	*3%*	*8%*
D	*8%*	*0.5*	*3%*	*8%*
E	*11%*	*1.0*	*3%*	*8%*

Calculating Treynor's Ratio for Each Portfolio

Portfolio A: $T_A = (10\% - 3\%) / 1.2 = 5.83$

Portfolio B: T_B=(12%−3%)/0.9=10.00
Portfolio C: T_C=(14%−3%)/1.5=7.33
Portfolio D: T_D=(8%−3%)/0.5=10.00
Portfolio E: TE=(11%−3%)/1.0=8.00

Interpreting the Results:

Portfolio B and Portfolio D both have the highest Treynor Ratios of 10.00, indicating that these portfolios are generating the highest return for each unit of market risk.

Portfolio A has a lower Treynor Ratio of 5.83, indicating that its return does not adequately compensate for the level of systematic risk.

Portfolio E also has a decent Treynor Ratio of 8.00, which places it in between Portfolio B/D and Portfolio A.

Portfolio C, with a Treynor Ratio of 7.33, is performing reasonably well, but it does not outperform Portfolios B or D, which have lower betas and higher risk-adjusted returns.

8.4 The Johnson Model (1968)

Johnson presented a model for measuring the performance of a portfolio of securities, known as the "Alpha coefficient." The concept of the model is based on finding the difference between two return measures:

The first measure represents the difference between the average return of the portfolio and the average risk-free return, which indicates the additional return. The second measure represents the product of the beta coefficient (β) and the difference between the average market return and the average return on the risk-free investment, known as the market premium. Thus, the Johnson model can be expressed as the following equation:

$$\alpha_p = (R_{pt} - R_F) - \beta_p \left[R_m - R_F\right] \qquad (41)$$

This forms a measure of the ability to achieve performance better than the market, and there are three cases. The following figure illustrates the different cases of portfolio managers' performance

Figure N°10: The first graphical measure of a portfolio according to Johnson

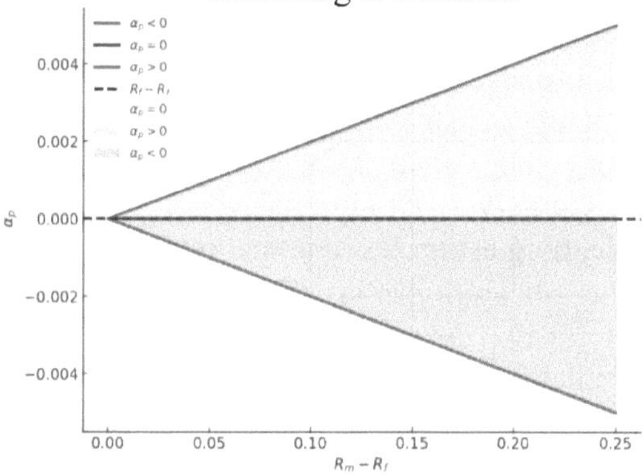

If α is positive, the manager can predict asset prices and make good selections whenever α_p is large.

If α_p is zero, the manager's selection may still be good, and they may achieve profits, but these profits (resulting from good selection) are exactly offset by management costs or transaction fees.

Criticisms of the Johnson Model (1968)

–Assumption that the relationship between returns and risk can be represented using the Beta coefficient (β): The Johnson Model relies on the Beta coefficient to establish the relationship between portfolio returns and market risk. However, Beta may not always accurately reflect market movements or investor behaviour. There are numerous other factors influencing portfolio performance, such as economic conditions or political changes, which are not accounted for by the model.

–Focus on past returns as a predictor of future success: The model heavily depends on historical returns for both the portfolio and risk-free assets. However, in volatile financial markets, past performance may not be a reliable indicator of future success. Generally, over-reliance on historical data can lead to inaccurate predictions of future performance.

–Neglect of associated costs and transaction fees: The Johnson Model implies that superior asset selection may be offset by management costs or transaction fees. In practice, these costs may not always be fully transparent or incorporated accurately in traditional models, leading to potentially misleading estimates of actual returns.

–Limited applicability in volatile or unstable markets: The model assumes that the relationship between returns and risk behaves predictably within the market. However, during periods of instability or financial crises, these relationships may not hold. Financial markets may experience irregular fluctuations that influence the model's outcomes in unforeseen ways.

–Performance measured only in comparison to the general market: The model compares portfolio performance to the broader market using risk-free returns as a benchmark. In some cases, this comparison may not be meaningful, particularly when dealing with specialised investment instruments or niche markets where the broader market comparison may not be applicable.

–Non-linear or unstable relationship between Alpha and Beta: In certain circumstances, the relationship between Alpha and Beta may not be consistent or linear. For example, in markets with significant volatility, the link between returns and risk may not follow a predictable pattern, undermining the reliability of the model's results.

Example N°34 : Using the Johnson Model (1968), calculate and interpret the Alpha coefficient for multiple portfolios based on the given data, and evaluate whether each portfolio has outperformed or underperformed the market.

Portfolio	*Annual Portfolio Return (Rp)*	*Annual Market Return (Rm)*	*Risk-Free Return (Rf)*	*Beta Coefficient (β)*
Portfolio 1	*12%*	*10%*	*3%*	*1.2*
Portfolio 2	*8%*	*10%*	*3%*	*0.9*
Portfolio 3	*14%*	*10%*	*3%*	*1.5*

1. *Calculate the Alpha for Each Portfolio:*

Portfolio 1: $\alpha_1=(12\%-3\%)-1.2\times(10\%-3\%)=0.6\%$ *Outperformed the market*

Portfolio 2: $\alpha_2=(8\%-3\%)-0.9\times(10\%-3\%)=-1.3\%$ *Underperformed the market*

Portfolio 3: $\alpha_3=(14\%-3\%)-1.5\times(10\%-3\%)=0.5\%$ *Outperformed the market*

8.5 The Fama Model

Fama presented a model for evaluating portfolio performance based on the comparison of portfolios with similar levels of risk. The model is based on predicting the expected market line, which illustrates the equilibrium relationship between expected return and risk for any portfolio.

The performance of a securities portfolio can be assessed based on three main components:

- Return from Selectivity: The performance of the portfolio under evaluation is represented by the selectivity rate, which is the difference between the return of the evaluated portfolio and the return of the risk-free portfolio and the market portfolio.

The return from selectivity is part of the total return of the securities portfolio. he selectivity rate quantifies the part of the portfolio's return that is attributable to the manager's skill in selecting securities. It shows how well the portfolio manager selects individual assets that outperform the market. The total return consists of two components: the first measures the return resulting from selecting the portfolio components, and the second measures the return corresponding to the portfolio's risk. (often represented by the market or the market index).

$$\text{Selectivity} = R_p - \left(R_f + \beta_p \times (R_m - R_f)\right) \quad (42)$$

- Return from Diversification: This is a measure that assesses the return added by diversification, and it can be divided into two types:
  - Return from net selectivity.
  - Return from diversification.

  If the portfolio is fully diversified, the total risk (σ) becomes equivalent to the systematic risk (β) of the market, as there is no unsystematic risk remaining. In such a case, the return resulting from diversification is zero because there is no additional diversification benefit left.
- Evaluating Risk: The portfolio's risk can be evaluated assuming the investor aims to bear a certain level of risk in the securities portfolio. Thus, the β coefficient, under this assumption, allows the total return, which compensates for the level of risk. In the figure N°11, we observe that a portfolio diversified simply achieves a certain level of market risk represented by (β_T)If the portfolio's risk equals the targeted risk ($\beta_A = \beta_T$), at this point, there is no risk for the manager.

However, if there is a difference between βT and β_A, the manager's risk is represented by the return that the manager must achieve to compensate for the risks of their decisions and the amount of risk B_A, which differs from the target risk level β_T .

In the case of a negative α, the manager's selection is poor, their ability to choose is weak, and the management costs are very high.

Figure N°11: illustrates the total performance return of the portfolio according to the Fama model.

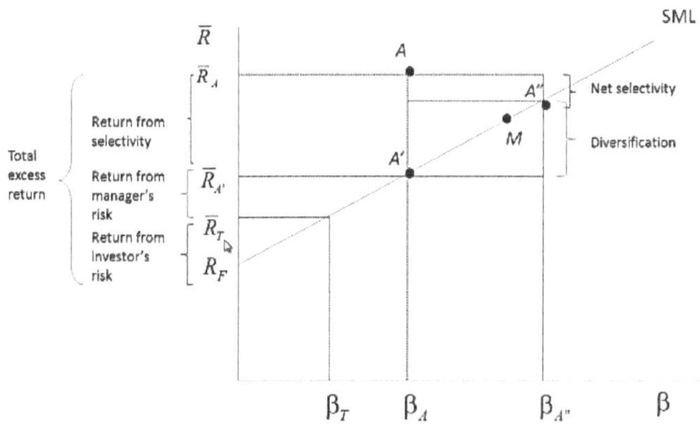

Visual Explanation Based on the Diagram:

- ✓ Representation Point A: represents the actual performance of the portfolio based on the manager's decisions. The return at this point is driven by the selectivity return, which is the part of the portfolio's return attributed to the manager's ability to select better-performing assets compared to the market. This is represented by the difference between the evaluated portfolio's return and the expected return based on the market's risk-return profile.
- ✓ Representation Point A': represents the expected performance of the portfolio based on the market return and the portfolio's beta coefficient (βp). the return that would be expected from the portfolio if it followed the

market's risk-return profile. Essentially, this return is what the portfolio would earn if it were fully aligned with the market's movements.

- ✓ Representation Point M: represents the market portfolio. This portfolio's return aligns perfectly with the Security Market Line (SML), meaning it provides an optimal risk-return trade-off based on the market's risk and return expectations. Return: The return at this point is the market return (R_m), which is the return that the market portfolio earns, and it is considered the benchmark for efficient portfolio performance.
- ✓ Representation: Point A" represents a portfolio that has achieved the optimal combination of both selectivity and diversification. It is the point where the portfolio manager has fully exploited their selectivity in selecting the best assets while also achieving complete diversification. As a result, the portfolio has maximized its performance by combining superior selection skills and reduced risk through diversification. The return at this point represents Net Selectivity, which is the additional return the portfolio achieves due to the manager's ability to select securities that outperform the market. This return is the additional value added by the portfolio manager beyond what would be expected based on the market's risk-return profile (as represented by the Security Market Line (SML)). In this case, the portfolio has successfully combined both selectivity and diversification, resulting in a return that surpasses the baseline market return, given the same level of risk.

Criticisms of the Fama Model :

- Efficient Market Hypothesis Assumption: The Fama Model assumes that markets are efficient and that prices always reflect all available information. However, in reality, markets can be inefficient due to anomalies such as overconfidence or market sentiment, which lead to prices deviating from their true value. This assumption limits the model's applicability when psychological or economic factors distort market movements.

- Unsystematic Risk: The Fama Model focuses primarily on systematic risk, represented by the beta coefficient (β), and overlooks unsystematic risks (risks specific to individual assets or portfolios) that may significantly impact portfolio performance. In real-world investing, unsystematic risks always exist, such as those arising from company-specific decisions or events.
- Overemphasis on Systematic Risk: The model relies heavily on comparing portfolios based on returns adjusted for systematic risk alone (i.e., market-related risks). However, this neglects the total risk of a portfolio, which includes both systematic and unsystematic components. This reduces the model's accuracy in providing a comprehensive assessment of a portfolio's overall risk.
- Lack of Flexibility in the Model: The Fama Model focuses on return and volatility based on market-related risks and does not consider specific economic changes or industry shifts. These factors may lead to return fluctuations that cannot be fully explained by market risk and return relationships, limiting the model's applicability in dynamic or unpredictable market conditions.
- Limitations of Beta: The model heavily depends on the beta coefficient as the main indicator of market-related risk. However, beta can be unstable over time, influenced by changes in economic conditions or shifts in market behaviour. This makes beta less reliable in

certain circumstances, which weakens its role as a stable measure of risk.

- Volatile Market Environments: The Fama Model relies on the Security Market Line (SML) to measure returns and risk. However, this model may not be flexible enough to account for market volatility or crises, where risk-return relationships can behave unpredictably. During such periods, the model may fail to accurately predict portfolio performance.
- Overlooking Transaction Costs and Fees: The Fama Model does not account for additional costs such as management fees, transaction costs, or tax implications. These costs can significantly impact the actual returns of a portfolio, yet the model fails to reflect these factors adequately.
- Failure to Address Optimal Asset Allocation: While the Fama Model compares returns to market risks, it does not provide solutions for optimal asset allocation to enhance returns or reduce risk within the portfolio. Approaches such as the Markowitz Model, which focus on optimal diversification, may be more effective in achieving a well-balanced portfolio that reduces total risk.

Example N°35: Using the Fama Model, evaluate the performance of three portfolios based on their selectivity, diversification, and risk, using the given data, and interpret the results.

Portfolio	*Portfolio Return (R_p)*	*Risk-Free Return (Rf)*	*Market Return (R_m)*	*Beta (β_p)*
Portfolio 1	*10%*	*2%*	*8%*	*1.1*
Portfolio 2	*15%*	*2%*	*8%*	*0.8*
Portfolio 3	*12%*	*2%*	*8%*	*1.3*

Let's calculate Return from Selectivity for each portfolio:

Portfolio 1: $Selectivity1=10\%-(2\%+1.1\times(8\%-2\%))=1.4\%$

The manager added 1.4% value through selectivity.
Portfolio 2: Selectivity2=15%−(2%+0.8×(8%−2%))=8.2%
The manager added 8.2% value through selectivity.Portfolio Selectivity3=12%−(2%+1.3×(8%−2%))=2.2%
The manager added 2.2% value through selectivity
Evaluation of Risk:

Portfolio	*Beta* (β_p)	*Target Beta* $(\beta_t = 1)$	*Interpretation*
Portfolio 1	*1.1*	*1*	*Slightly more risk than the market.*
Portfolio 2	*0.8*	*1*	*Less risk than the market.*
Portfolio 3	*1.3*	*1*	*More risk than the market.*

Conclusion:

Portfolio 1 has a selectivity return of 1.4%. It performed slightly better than expected based on its risk, though it carries slightly more risk than the market.

Portfolio 2 has an exceptional selectivity return of 8.2%, outperforming both the market and the risk-free investment. Despite its lower risk (beta of 0.8), it still provided excellent returns, suggesting good manager skill in asset selection.

Portfolio 3 has a selectivity return of 2.2%, which is decent, but it also carries more risk (beta of 1.3), meaning the manager needs to generate higher returns to justify this additional risk.

8.6 Henrikson-Merton Model

The Henrikson-Merton model suggests that performance measurement resulting from the manager's asset selection should be separated from the measurement based on the manager's ability to match the market. Asset selection serves as a reference for the manager’s competence in choosing assets with superior performance relative to those in the market, while accounting for their associated risks. The model is expressed as follows:

- R_p: Portfolio return at time t.
- R_{xt}: Risk-free rate at time t.
- R_{mt}: Market return at time t.
- D: A dummy variable that takes the value of 1 when the portfolio's return exceeds the risk-free rate, and 0 otherwise.
- $P^t\varepsilon$: Residual return.
- $P\alpha$, β_P, γ_p: Model parameters.

Thus, if the market return is lower than the risk-free rate, the portfolio's beta will be P_β or $P{+}\gamma pP\beta P + \gamma_p\ P_\beta$ if it is the opposite. The coefficient αP measures the manager's skill in selecting assets, while γ_p measures the manager's ability to match the market. If γ_p is positive, it indicates that the manager is effectively following the market. If γ_p is negative, it suggests that the manager holds valuable information but is applying it in an irrational manner.

Criticisms of the Henrikson-Merton Model:

- Complexity of Calculation: The model involves several parameters, such as P_β, γ_p , and α_P, which require precise data on market returns, residual returns, and asset selection. This can make the model complex to apply in real-world scenarios, especially when the required data is not readily available or is difficult to obtain.
- Assumption of Market Matching: The model assumes that a manager's performance can be directly attributed to their ability to "match" the market. However, this may not always be the case in real-world scenarios where external factors like market volatility, investor sentiment, and geopolitical risks can influence the market in ways that are difficult for any manager to predict or match.
- Overemphasis on Risk Matching: The model places significant emphasis on the manager's ability to match

the market. This could potentially undermine the value of active management strategies that aim to outperform the market rather than simply replicate its performance. In reality, the goal of portfolio management may be to achieve superior returns while taking on an acceptable level of risk, which may not always align with the model's focus on market matching.

- Interpretation of γ_p : The interpretation of the $\gamma p \gamma_P \gamma p$ parameter as an indicator of whether the manager is matching the market or using information irrationally can be subjective. A negative $\gamma p \gamma_P \gamma p$ does not necessarily indicate irrationality—it could simply reflect the manager's contrarian strategy or different risk preferences. The model might not fully capture these nuanced strategies.
- Lack of Adaptability in Different Market Conditions: The model assumes a stable and predictable relationship between the manager's asset selection and market performance. However, in highly volatile or non-efficient markets, this relationship might not hold, limiting the model's applicability in crisis situations or emerging markets.

Example N° 36: Let's apply the Henrikson-Merton Model to a hypothetical portfolio:

- Portfolio Return R_p=12%.
- Risk-Free Rate R_{xt}=3%.
- Market Return R_{mt}=8%.
- β_P=1.2 (Portfolio's beta)
- γ_p=0.5 (Market matching factor)
- D=1 (since $R_p > R_{xt}$)

The value of α_P (manager's skill in selecting assets) is calculated using the following formula:

$\alpha_P = Rp - (R_{xt} + \beta_P \times (R_{mt} - R_{xt})) = 12\% - (3\% + 1.2 \times (8\% - 3\%)) = 3\%$

Thus, α_P=3% which indicates that the manager added 3% value through their asset selection.
Since γ_p is positive, it indicates that the manager is effectively matching the market. This suggests that the manager is following the market trends and adjusting the portfolio accordingly.

8.7 Obstacles in Performance Measurement

The methods we use to measure performance have recently been the subject of criticism, which can be classified into five key elements:

- Comparison of Portfolio Performance Relative to the Benchmark:
  Comparing the performance of a portfolio, which adjusts returns to account for risk, to a benchmark is practically incorrect. The performance of the benchmark is not equivalent to the performance of the portfolio when it comes to measurement. The benchmark incurs some costs, such as reinvesting profits, selling stocks to meet redemption requests from clients, and rebalancing the portfolio to account for changes in the performance of the benchmark index that the portfolio is attempting to replicate. All of these are opportunities that involve costs, which reduce the performance of the benchmark. In order to make a proper comparison with the evaluated portfolio's performance, these factors must be taken into account.
- Portfolio Return Does Not Reflect the Manager's True Ability:
  Although the return achieved by the portfolio over time can be measured precisely, this does not reflect the manager's true ability or skill. The performance measured does not necessarily account for the manager's decision-making and adaptability in managing the portfolio.
- The Return Measure Over Time:
  In practice, the rate of return achieved works by forming

an observation that falls within the distribution of return rates obtained over a larger number of successive periods. This only becomes apparent after observing a series of time periods, which allows us to discern the line between short-term fluctuations and the manager's true capabilities.

- Unrealistic Assumptions About Risk-Free Rates and Borrowing Rates:
  It is unreasonable to assume that risk-free rates and borrowing rates are equal. The assumption that they are equal would require setting an excessively high benchmark for comparing portfolios that bear the highest risks. Such an assumption does not reflect the true dynamics of risk and return in the real market.
- Performance Indicators Assumed by Models: All performance indicators, particularly those used by Treynor and Johnson, assume Dow-like features of stability which do not necessarily exist. These models often overlook the inherent volatility and uncertainty present in real market conditions.
- Measurement Errors in Market Return Rates: Measuring market return rates can contain errors, and there is likely an effect on performance measurement that should not be neglected when comparing portfolios. These errors can distort the true performance of the portfolios being compared, leading to inaccurate conclusions about their relative performance.

References

abozzi, F. J., & Modigliani, F. (2001). *Foundations of financial markets and institutions* (3rd ed.). Prentice Hall.

Al-Hanawi, M. S. (2003). *Investment in securities*. Dar Al-Jami'ah for publishing and distribution. Alexandria.

Al-Hanawi, M. S., & Ibrahim, J. (2005). *The stock exchange: Theory and practice*. Dar Al-Jami'ah. Alexandria.

Al-Shabib, D. K. (2010). *Investment portfolio management*. Dar Al-Masirah. 1st ed. Amman.

Al-Tamimi, A. F. (2010). *Financial markets: Framework for organizing and evaluating instruments*. Dar Al-Yazouri. Amman.

Bani Hani, H. (2002). *Financial markets: Nature, organization, and derivative instruments*. Dar Al-Kindi. Amman, Jordan.

Ben Suleiman, M. (2005). *Regulating modern financial markets*. Knows Ashbilia, Vol. 1. 1st ed. Riyadh.

Bodie, Z., Kane, A., & Marcus, A. J. (2014). *Investments* (10th ed.). McGraw-Hill Education.

Dagher, M. M. (2005). *Financial markets: Institutions, securities, exchanges*. Al-Shorouk for production and distribution. No edition.

Elton, E. J., & Gruber, M. J. (2013). *Modern portfolio theory and investment analysis* (9th ed.). Wiley.

Fabozzi, F. J., Jones, F. J., Fabozzi, F. A., & Mann, S. V. (2021). *Foundations of global financial markets and institutions* (5th ed.). Pearson.

Fadly, H. (2004). *Management of financial portfolios for others: A comparative legal study*. Dar Al-Jami'ah Al-Jadidah. Algeria.

Fama, E. F., & French, K. R. (1993). Common risk factors in the returns on stocks and bonds. *Journal of Financial Economics, 33*(1), 3–56. https://doi.org/10.1016/0304-405X(93)90023-5

Fared, N., & Abdel, J. (2003). *Investment in securities*. Dar Al-Jami'ah. Alexandria.

Gruber, M. J. (2010). *Investments and portfolio performance*. World Scientific.

Hamad, T. A. (2003). *Risk management: Individuals, departments, companies, and banks*. Ain Shams University. Dar Al-Jami'ah. Alexandria.

Hanafi, A. G. (2001). *Essentials of investment in the stock exchange (stocks, bonds, investment documents, options)*. Dar Al-Jami'ah Al-Jadidah for publishing. Alexandria.

Hindi, M. I. (1999). *Investment funds for small and large savers*. Masha'at Al-Ma'arif. Alexandria.

Hindi, M. I. (1999). *Investment tools in capital markets*. Arab Modern Office. Alexandria.

Hindi, M. I. (2011). *Commercial banking management*. Arab Modern Office. Alexandria.

Hussein, E. (2008). *Financial markets*. Osama for publishing and distribution. 1st ed. Amman.

Ibrahim, J. (2009). *Essentials of investment in securities and stock exchanges*. Dar Al-Kitab Al-Hadith for production and distribution. Algeria.

Jensen, M. C. (1968). The performance of mutual funds in the period 1945–1964. *Journal of Finance, 23*(2), 389–416. https://doi.org/10.1111/j.1540-6261.1968.tb00815.

Khalaf, F. H. (2006). *Financial and monetary markets*. Aware for modern books. 1st ed. Jordan.

Khodari, M. A. (n.d.). *How to learn the stock market in 24 hours*. Etrak for publishing and distribution. 2nd ed.

Obaid, S. T. (n.d.). *Investment in securities*. Ain Shams Library. Cairo.

Ross, S. A. (1976). The arbitrage theory of capital asset pricing. *Journal of Economic Theory, 13*(3), 341–360. https://doi.org/10.1016/0022-0531(76)90002-1

Ryan, T. P. (Ed.). (2006). *Portfolio analysis: Advanced topics in performance measurement, risk, and attribution*. Risk Books.

Sahnoun, M. (2003). *Monetary and banking economics*. Dar Beha'a for publishing and distribution. Constantine, Algeria.

Shamoun, S. (n.d.). *The stock market and the Algerian stock exchange*. Dar Homa for publishing and distribution. Algeria.

Sharpe, W. F. (1964). Capital asset prices: A theory of market equilibrium under conditions of risk. *Journal of Finance, 19*(3), 425–442. https://doi.org/10.1111/j.1540-6261.1964.tb02865.x

Shawwa, F. M. (2008). *Investment in the stock exchange: Theoretical and scientific foundations*. Dar Wail for publishing and distribution. 1st ed. Amman, Jordan.

Sultan, I., & Abdel, J. (2002). *Analysis and evaluation of securities*. Dar Al-Jami'ah. Alexandria.

Tawfiq, J. A. (n.d.). *Fundamentals of financial management*. Dar Al-Nahda Al-Arabia for printing and publishing. Lebanon.

Treynor, J. L. (1965). How to rate management of investment funds. *Harvard Business Review, 43*(1), 63–75.

FSC
www.fsc.org
MIX
Papier | Fördert
gute Waldnutzung
FSC® C083411

Kolibri 360 GmbH
Ferdinand-Jühlke-Straße 7
99095 Erfurt, Deutschland
produktsicherheit@kolibri360.de

Druck:
CPI Druckdienstleistungen GmbH
im Auftrag der
Kolibri 360 GmbH
Ferdinand-Jühlke-Str. 7
99095 Erfurt